ST. MARY'S, Little Crosby

"Catholicity survived in Lancashire not only because of the staunchness proper to its people, the tenacity with which they cling to old traditions, but because the Faith itself is in the very marrow of their being".

M.E. Francis.

(Mrs. Mary Blundell of Crosby 1859 - 1930).

ST. MARY'S Little Crosby
A History

Brian Plumb

Published in Great Britain in 1997 by
The Friends of St Mary's, Little Crosby

ISBN 0 9531327 0 6

Designed and Printed in Great Britain by
Sefton Neighbourhood Initiative Project (SNIP),
Deerbarn Drive, Old Roan, Liverpool L30 8SA

Foreword

by His Grace the Archbishop of Liverpool

I have often felt that we could re-name the Acts of the Apostles 'The Second Book of the Story of Jesus now living in his body the Church'. I think this is how St. Luke might have described the work. That story of Jesus in his body which is the Church continues through all ages. It could also be described as the account of the activities of the Holy Spirit in every time and place. This history of St. Mary's, Little Crosby, is a great and inspiring chapter in its wider history.

✝ Patrick Kelly,
Archbishop of Liverpool

Contents

Introduction

It is a fact of history that on 7th September, 1847, the church of St. Mary at Little Crosby was solemnly consecrated. The following day it was opened to the public. The details of its building, the faith and devotion of those by whom it was built and those for whom it was built, even the land on which it stands, is all so inextricably mingled with the politics and laws of England itself, that to explain the one is, very often, to confront the other.

To give some historical account we must retreat not a hundred and fifty years to the reign of Queen Victoria and the opening of the railway from Liverpool to Southport, but four hundred and fifty years to the Reformation and all the turbulence and intolerance that accompanied it.

To do so is quite a daunting task, not least because so much of it has already been done before, and what is more has been done very skilfully. The work of Frank Tyrer who died in 1984 stands pre-eminent in this respect, whether published or still in manuscript. The research done by Brian Whitlock Blundell, fascinating in its wealth of detail and well worthy of publication in its own right, has been made available to me without reserve.

Secondly, it often seems incomprehensible to the present generation that there was a time when individuals and entire families literally endured dungeon, fire and sword in defiance of laws that sometimes carried the death penalty against their most fervently held convictions. There are also well-meaning people who think that reviving memories of unhappy events is a hindrance to Christian unity if not an affront to Christian charity. But if only what is good had ever been told we should never have heard of the betrayal by Judas, the denial by Peter or the conversion of Paul. Each must decide according to conscience, but it is no service to ecumenism to judge the events of former days by the standards we enjoy today.

I gladly acknowledge assistance received from Mgr. Breen and Canon Daley. Mrs. M.C. Barnes, the head teacher has also been generous with her time. Mollie Gilligan, Teresa Jones and her sister Gertrude, and Bob Wright have all dealt patiently and sympathetically with my innumerable questions, and Tom Gradwell would have shared his knowledge and experience but was prevented from doing so by illness. Mr. and Mrs. Austin Varney and Mr. and Mrs. Whitlock Blundell have provided me with hospitality as well as encouragement, and the staff in the local history department of Crosby Library have been extremely helpful on six occasions if not seven. Bernard Ball of Warrington has devoted hours of his time to word-processing my original text, but the final responsibility for what is written rests with me.

I can only repeat what the famous historian Hugh Tootell, alias Charles Dodd wrote about his epic work. "After all the search I have made, the work will still be imperfect". But I can add that I believe I have made use of the best material and resources available to me.

So against a background of ever changing national and ecclesiastical rules and regulations, an ancient family and village community, intense love of environment and tradition and unwavering fidelity to the Universal Church is the body of our story. The never-failing grace of God is its soul.

Brian Plumb.

Feast of the Ascension, 1997.

CHAPTER 1

Kings, Queens and Countryfolk

"The good will be firm and suffer, the lukewarm will fail if they find none to help them, the greater part will stray like sheep without a shepherd."

Catherine of Aragon to Pope Paul III, 1535.

With extraordinary perception the rejected spouse of King Henry VIII wrote these words in a letter to the Pope informing him about events that had overtaken her in the very last months of her life. Four years earlier, unable to bear Henry a son, she had been humiliated and divorced. Had she lived four months more she might have added that the woman who had displaced her had been humiliated and beheaded.

In February 1531 the King had repudiated Papal authority and declared himself Head of the Church in this realm. Under pain of treason, he demanded the public acquiescence of all his nobles and officials not only for his newly declared status but also later for the recognition of his second marriage and the legitimacy of the daughter born of it. The majority had complied without a murmur but there had been some notable exceptions. Before Catherine's own death in January 1536, John Fisher, Bishop of Rochester, Thomas More, the Lord Chancellor, three Carthusians, a Bridgettine and the Vicar of Isleworth had all chosen to be killed rather than deny the primacy of the Pope or the permanence of the marriage bond.(1)

Dissolution of Monasteries

Before 1531 Henry had tried to persuade Rome to annul his marriage. In this he had been supported by Thomas Wolsey who as Papal Legate, Cardinal Arch-bishop of York and Lord Chancellor had attained as high an office in Church and State as anyone could. That Wolsey had failed to obtain the King's desire is well known. But he had employed as secretary, Thomas Cromwell, an unimportant man but a very clever one who was quick to learn. Whenever Wolsey wanted to build himself a palace or endow a college he would, with all the skill of a great administrator, close a monastery here or a convent there, or unite two separate communities. The revenues from the suppressed houses and their lands would then be transferred to Wolsey's own coffers. Cromwell knew all about this and how it could be done. What is more, he knew that the King was constantly in need of money, and with his vast knowledge of the wealth of the monasteries, he hinted at a solution. (2)

While Catherine was writing to the Pope, the French ambassador in London was also writing "What the King intends to do is usurp part of the Church goods and distribute the remainder to noblemen.........the King is very covetous of the goods of the Church which he already considers his patrimony."

As far as can be calculated there were at that time 822 religious houses, great or small, throughout England, 353 of men and 469 of women. Within four years 716 of them were suppressed, their revenues confiscated and their inhabitants made vagrants. At Glastonbury in Somerset and at Whalley in Lancashire, the Abbots were hanged at their own gates. There was of course considerable reaction by the laity. (3)

Pilgrimage of Grace

In the autumn of 1536 ten thousand marched in protest through Lincolnshire but disbanded after a King's messenger denied there would be any confiscations but warned that argument would be dealt with as treason. The northern counties raised thirty thousand men, many of them armed, under the leadership of Robert Aske who insisted they were pilgrims supporting Christ's Holy Church, not rebels protesting against taxes. At Doncaster they met with three thousand soldiers. There, a promise was given to them that their petition would be presented to the King. So, with profound reverence for the Monarchy and the willing acceptance of the abjectness required of a subject, Aske advised his followers to disperse. (4)

But the King was furious that none of them had been hanged and said a slur had been cast upon his honour. Reprisals most fearful were exacted. In February, 1537 nine persons, three of them clerics, were hanged. At Hull, two priests (later beatified) were hanged. A further forty executions took place in Yorkshire or Durham. In Lincolnshire thirty-four persons were hanged. Twelve suffered at Tyburn, the Vicar of Louth among them. Others were beheaded on Tower Hill or burned at Smithfield. Two monks and twelve laymen from Lancashire were executed as were seventy-four people at Carlisle. The whole nation reverberated with terror until on 12 July, Aske himself was executed at York. (5)

The Place of the Cross

But what, it might be asked, had all this to do with Little Crosby (Place of the Cross), a lonely spot on the West Lancashire coast, six and a half miles north of Liverpool. Since 1362 it had been the manor of the ancient family of Blundell of Crosby. From time immemorial it had been a small township in the parish of Sefton whose church of St. Helen stood two miles to the south-east. And it lay within the diocese of Lichfield whose bishop lived the best part of a hundred miles to the south. (6)

Sefton Church circa 1900

The glib might reply to this question by saying it hardly made any difference at all because little if anything changed very much. And over the subsequent four hundred and fifty years Catholicism has never ceased to be practised there. None but Catholic sacraments have ever been administered. Mass has been celebrated unfailingly if at times surreptitiously. Mary has always been honoured, the faithful departed have received Catholic burial (often at dead of night) and been remembered in prayer. The Blundell family has remained at Crosby Hall and the authority of the Pope has never been challenged. (7)

Ancient documents describe Little Crosby as a number of cottages with closes strung on either side of a lane, enclosed by a gate. There were meadows and pastures, poultry farming and good potato harvests, said to have originated from tubers cast ashore from a wreck off Formby. Some of the inhabitants were fishermen and it would appear there were about forty-four families. (8)

Remote as it was, it is probable that news of the suppression of the Augustinian Hermits Friary at Warrington, the Benedictine Priory at Upholland and the Augustinian Canons Priory at Burscough reached it. But the structure of society at the time was undoubtedly the source of much, if not all of its incorruptibility. The land-owning classes exercised authority over all - wife, children, servants, tenants and everything within their sway, including religion. But what Professor John Bossy calls "the remorseless constancy of the Blundells" is unique in the annals of

English Catholicism. Some great houses have indeed made noble and often heroic contributions to the preservation of the Faith, those of Howard, Stonor, Talbot, Towneley and Petre to name but a few. But as modest country squires, the contribution of the Blundells of Crosby is as interesting as it is unvacillating. (9)

I Sought Peace in All Things

The name Blundell, derived presumably from Blondel (the fair one) was first used by Robert who came from Ainsdale in the 13th century. His son, Nicholas owned lands in Ainsdale, Ravenmeols, Walton, Bold, Great Crosby, Little Crosby and Liverpool which was then only a tiny village. Later the manor of Ditton near Widnes was added to their possessions. His son, David we might say was the first Blundell of Crosby. By marrying Agnes Molyneux, sister of Sir John Molyneux who as Lord of the manor of Little Crosby died in 1362 when all his children had predeceased him, David Blundell founded the dynasty which still exists. Having been foresters in the reign of King John their Coat of Arms consists of ten silver billets (sectioned logs) on a background of sable (black). The motto IN OMNIBUS REQUIEM QUAESIVI (I sought peace in all things) has proved to be poignantly accurate for centuries. (10)

David and Agnes had a son Nicholas who was succeeded by his son Henry. The property passed through the male line for seven generations to Henry, who was killed at Flodden in 1513. Twice married, he had twenty-six children which perhaps explains why the name Blundell is so frequently encountered all along the Mersey from Southport to Liverpool. At the age of ten, Henry Blundell (1517-1556) succeeded, and married Anne Leyland of Morleys near Leigh in south Lancashire. There might have been little to disturb them subsequent to the royal divorce but their son Richard (1536-1591) and his wife, Anne Starkie of Stretton near Warrington, had to contend with the full force of the Reformation.

Considering that Richard had had a rural upbringing, uninfluenced by the affairs of State, and that his early knowledge of persecution must have been gained from history and not experience, it is all the more amazing that he rose to be such a valiant confessor of the Faith. National events shaped his fate but his example ensured that his son and successor William Blundell (1560-1638) was known as "the Recusant", that is from the Latin Recuso "I refuse". (11)

Reformation

While Henry VIII rejected the primacy of the Pope and suppressed the monasteries he never interfered with doctrine. Neither would he permit others to do so. In Henry's reign it was just as possible to be put to death for denying the Real Presence in the Blessed Sacrament of the Altar as it was for acknowledging the authority of the Pope. But when Henry died in 1547 and was followed by his son, Edward VI who reigned for only six years and died at the age of seventeen, radical changes were introduced. Families who had become extremely rich after the dissolution of the monasteries, either by rewards from the King for loyalty or through buying monastic property from the Crown at about half its true value, entrenched their positions. Realising that to resubmit to Rome could well mean surrendering their wealth, they acquired a decidedly anti-Catholic position, and for long before the divorce religion had had its non-compliants. Lancashire itself contained all manner of opposing elements from Puritanism to witchcraft. Greatly influenced by the teachings of Martin Luther and John Calvin, the State religion assumed a definite Protestant complexion which was proclaimed in its prayers, ceremonies, writings and laws. The Mass and the sacraments, veneration of Our Lady, the saints and prayers for the dead were all rejected as superstitious. Eventually these changes would be enforced by law. (12)

During the five year reign of Mary, an ardent Catholic and eldest child of Henry VIII, attempts were made to repair the break between England and Rome. Her cousin, Cardinal Pole, was made Archbishop of Canterbury and he publicly absolved the Nation. Somewhat guardedly word was given that monastic property need not be repossessed, but Westminster Abbey was restored to the Benedictines.

Then the severity of law was invoked against any who had assisted with her parents' divorce and in her own degradation from Princess. Those who had participated in a plot to dethrone her in favour of Lady Jane Grey, a tragic girl who hardly knew what was happening, were condemned for treason. Others whose preaching and religious ministrations had assisted the changes were also condemned. Once again burnings and beheadings horrified the people as approximately two hundred and seventy three people perished. To her critics Mary was and is Bloody Mary. To the dispassionate she was a monarch of her time and a Tudor to boot. (13)

On 17 November, 1558 Queen Mary died and was succeeded by her half-sister, Elizabeth who believed that Catholics only regarded her as "the illegitimate fruit of an adulterous connexion" (Bishop Goss). Religious discord flared up immediately. She directed that the host be not elevated at Mass. Every bishop of a diocese in England went to prison or into exile, though not before Oglethorpe of Carlisle had agreed to crown her. Canterbury was vacant at the time and Archbishop Heath of York refused to perform the Coronation ceremony.

Queen Elizabeth made her position quite clear. A nation divided was undesirable if not ungovernable and religious division was the most undesirable of all. As she favoured the Protestant way, the year 1559 found Parliament almost absorbed in anti-Catholic legislation. The Act of Supremacy excluded all foreign jurisdiction and proclaimed the Queen supreme in all matters ecclesiastical. This Act was to be enforced upon oath. The Act of Uniformity, although passed in the Lords by only three votes, abolished the Mass and imposed the Book of Common Prayer upon every congregation in the land. "Both Acts bristled with sanctions for the disobedient" (Hughes). First offenders were forbidden to hold any public office and suffer loss of goods or chattels. A second offence could mean loss of property and imprisonment for life. A third offence was high treason. As to the Act of Uniformity, "clergy who break this law by refusing to use the new Prayer Book, or use any other rite, or who speak in derogation of the book, forfeit a whole years income and go to prison for six months." Further offences carried penalties up to being imprisoned for life and there were severe penalties to discourage lay critics. "For all who speak or write in derogation....or hinder performance of the services.... loss of all goods and chattels and life imprisonment." And all were now commanded by law to attend their parish church every Sunday and Holy Day or pay a fine of twelve pence. To assist at Mass meant six months imprisonment for a first offence, twelve months for a second, and life for the third. In 1563 these penalties were increased and a new crime, that of defending the Pope's spiritual jurisdiction came into being. (14)

Resistance

It is said that in south-west Lancashire there was little enthusiasm for, and much resentment against, such harsh measures. However, three quarters of the parochial clergy did not resist the new laws. Commissioners, clerical and lay were nominated to supervise implementation but other than public church services there is, around Crosby at least, the distinct impression of laxity if not of chaos among the overseers. What prosecutions there were seem to have emanated from the zeal of the common informer.

By 1566 Crosby Hall with its priests hiding-hole had been identified as a centre of resistance and there is evidence of pre-reformation priests ministering there. James Hargreaves, Vicar of Blackburn, and ten other priests south of the Ribble refused the Oath of Supremacy and became itinerants. They moved quietly from place to place encouraging the faithful. One of their number, Peter Jackson, who sometimes visited Little Crosby, and who died at Speke in 1599 was the last of the old Marian clergy to serve in Lancashire.

Michael Trappes-Lomax, an early 20th century historian wrote "It was possible to go from Little Crosby to Lancaster without leaving Catholic ground. A brief examination of the map shows how easy it would be to pass on the priests from manor-house to manor-house in very short journeys. A priest travelling, for example, from Cheshire might cross the Mersey in the neighbourhood of Liverpool and make his first call on the Norris family at Speke. From there he might ride to Crosby to minister to the Blundells and then on to the Irelands at Lydiate or the Molyneux at Sefton. An easy ride would bring him to Scarisbrick Hall where he would stay with the Scarisbricks who would then commend him to the Heskeths of Rufford. Here he would be within a short distance of Salmesbury and after resting there he might follow the line of the Catholic manor-houses in the Ribble valley through the Trough of Bowland to Lancaster and the north, or he might make for Preston where he would find many Catholic houses, journeying on by way of the Catholic squires of the Fylde to the Allens at Rossall." (15)

"It must be emphasised that even in the so-called Catholic areas, Catholics were in a minority." (Hilton, Catholic Lancashire p.11).

Without bishops or any defined authority these old recusants were left to manage as best they could. Also in 1566 Laurence Vaux appeared hereabouts. A native of Blackrod and an Oxford graduate, as warden of the Manchester Collegiate Church he refused to conform in 1559. His Catechism became one of the principal means of information and instruction for his co-religionists. He produced an oath of loyalty to the Pope which was signed by numerous people including Sir Richard

Part of a map as used by Nicholas Blundell

Molyneux of Sefton and his entire family, by Sir William Norris of Speke, John Molyneux of Melling, Robert Blundell of Ince and Richard Blundell of Crosby and two former priests of Sefton parish. By 1568 this Richard Blundell was in prison. By 1569 it looked as if the Pilgrimage of Grace was about to reassemble. (16)

In November, 1569 a group in the northern counties rallied support and marched on Durham. High Mass was celebrated in the cathedral for the first time in ten years and contemporary accounts say it was crowded to the very doors. The assembly professed loyalty to the Queen but pleaded for the restoration of "the ancient customs and liberties of the old and Catholic religion." There was a lot of support but no chance of success and after marching as far as Tadcaster they were routed. A vengeance of six or seven hundred executions settled it. But there were some people who claimed that Mary Queen of Scots should replace Elizabeth as

Queen. Mary, a daughter of Margaret, the sister of Henry VIII, was to some peoples thinking, his closest living legitimate relative. Apart from, wittingly or otherwise, paving the way for that unfortunate woman's execution, because Elizabeth then considered her very presence to be a threat, they also gave grounds to those who said Catholics were traitors and not to be trusted with civil liberties. (17)

In February 1570 Pope Pius V published *Regnans in Excelsis,* a copy of which was audaciously nailed to the door of the Bishop of London's palace. By it Elizabeth was pronounced excommunicated and her subjects, in conscience, released from allegiance. But it made no mention of her illegitimate birth and gave no support to the Queen of Scots. Neither was it anywhere suggested that Catholics must rebel nor was there any appeal to Catholic sovereigns to make war against her. About this declaration and its relevance there has never ceased to be controversy. Years later an important Government official said that Catholics had given no support to England's enemies and went on to give examples of their loyalty. (18)

Recusancy

In Elizabethan Lancashire, Henry Stanley, fourth Earl of Derby, was responsible for the administration of civil law and, since the creation of the diocese in 1541, the Bishops of Chester regulated religious observance. It is probably true that their indifference prevented much of the county from turning to violence during the unrest in 1569. It is certainly true that Lord Derby had no great desire to harass his friends and neighbours. His own household was reputedly a nest of non-communicants and plotters. Two of his sons were thought to be involved in a scheme to spirit Mary Queen of Scots away to the Isle of Man and lead a rebellion from there, Glaseour, the chamberlain at Chester who had dealings with Derby over legal matters was suspected of being a secret Catholic.

Of Chester it is written "its bishops could make little contact with the rough people of Lancashire and it is doubtful whether they even desired to do so." From 1561 to 1577 William Downham was Bishop of Chester. He had been chaplain to Elizabeth before her accession but as bishop he was so inactive that in 1568 the Privy Council, complaining that Lancashire was a sink of popery, ordered the Bishop of Carlisle to make a visitation. He was horrified at what he found, but out of 800 named offenders only 200 were brought to court of which only 11 paid recusancy fines. The faith of the Lancashire Catholics was very strong. (19)

To deal with such cases the Bishop of Chester had four resources:

1 The Consistory

2 The Visitation Court

3 The Rural Deans

4 The Ecclesiastical Commissioners

Despite these and the many sanctions at his disposal, it would appear that, put in simple language, it cost twenty pounds to collect a fine of one pound. Furthermore the court apparitor was described as a corrupt person, a common briber and an extortioner. Another official was accused of fornication by a parishioner. It was by way of this state of chronic ineptitude that Richard Blundell found himself in prison in 1568 on a charge of harbouring priests. Who these priests were and what we know of them will be revealed in a later section, suffice to say that around Crosby there were several. Richard Blundell was eventually released because the Council could not agree on a policy towards the recusant gentry. From time to time token trials were arranged and some sort of example created. But for the time being Mr. Blundell went home to Little Crosby and accumulated a library of Catholic literature. (20)

Martyrdom

The Elizabethan Government made a couple of serious miscalculations when legislating against religion. Firstly, it was never anticipated that the ferocious laws against recusants would be resisted so vehemently, especially by the gentry. These laws caused government agents a good deal of embarrassment to enforce, to say nothing of the expense. And the tenantry invariably followed the landlord's lead. It was in such an atmosphere that no action was taken against Richard Blundell in 1586 when yet again, this time by the officious curate of Sefton, he was reported for harbouring a priest. Other reasons have often been put forward to explain the strength of recusancy such as poor access for central authority, powerful bonds between families and neighbours and, surprisingly perhaps in view of the foregoing, some genuine sympathy from the clergy of the Established Church. The informer, Thomas Bell who flourished hereabouts at that time, apart from claiming to know of ninety-three safe houses, considered that Anglican clergy who were reticent about prosecuting papists were equally deserving of exposure. But the most vital factor in the preservation of real Catholicism, as opposed to mere recusancy, was that the flow of native vocations to the priesthood never failed. This was the Government's second miscalculation but in this matter there would be no turning of blind-eyes. (21)

Queen Elizabeth and her advisers imagined that as the older generation of Catholic-minded clergy and laity died out then Catholicism would expire too. In this they were to be proved wrong but extremely spiteful. Yet the reason their thinking was thwarted was only a secondary product, a sort of afterthought in the mind of its animator.

William Allen (1532-1594) was a native of Rossall, Lancashire, and a graduate of Oriel College, Oxford. Refusing to take the new Oaths in 1559 he removed to the University of Louvain. He well understood the conditions to which Catholicism in England had been reduced, a state which incidentally he thought would be only temporary, and he knew that good theological literature was required to sustain it. At Douai he gathered a group of academics so expert that eventually they produced an English translation of the Bible, but that is another matter. Training priests was never his intention, but many young Englishmen begged him to do so, in fact more applied than could be dealt with. Douai received its first students in 1568 and held its first ordinations in 1574. Then these seminary priests, as they were called returned home to support the faithful and reconcile the lapsed. Later Allen founded similar colleges in Rome and Valladolid and was created Cardinal and Protector of the English Mission. (22)

The laws passed against these priests were truly draconian. All ordained since 24 June, 1559 by authority of the See of Rome were required to leave the country or be punished as traitors. Section after Section prescribed the direst penalties until in the end to enter the Country, to be in it or to remain in it carried the death penalty in its most excruciating form of being hanged, drawn and quartered. All who sheltered or in any way aided such priests were to be hanged as felons. But, if any of these so condemned would take the Oath acknowledging the Queen to be supreme in matters of religion, nothing in the Act was to apply to them. One of these priest-martyrs was Crosby's very own Blessed Laurence Johnson, the first of the many Lancashire Martyrs. (23)

Blessed Laurence Johnson

Like many of the missionary priests working in a life threatening environment he sometimes used an alias which accounts for some sources referring to him as Laurence Richardson. His father was Robert Johnson of Crosby, his mother was Margaret Blundell of Ince Blundell, related indirectly to the Blundells of Crosby. His birthplace, a farm near what is now Old Farm Road has been demolished but a lintel was removed to Moorside Park. He was educated at Crosby Grammar School and Brasenose College, Oxford, therefore he must have subscribed to the obligatory Oaths. But considering his antecedents and the fact that his sister, Helen, was imprisoned for recusancy in Salford Gaol in 1582, we might question how much of a Protestant he had been. He entered the college at Douai in 1573 and was ordained priest on 23 May, 1577.

On 23 July of that year he arrived at Park House near Chorley, home of Mr. Richard Houghton. Under the guise of schoolmaster he performed his priestly duties throughout that district. Preserved among the State papers is a letter from one of his converts, Christopher Hodgson, who wrote "It is not as Mr. Johnson that I address you but as my father who brought me out of the land of Egypt and slavery."

We do not know if he ever came to Little Crosby but he visited his kinsmen at Ince Blundell, one of whom, the young Robert Blundell he sent to Rheims to try his vocation. Indirectly this brought about Laurence Johnson's death. He was requested, as an act of charity, to go to London to collect a sum of money owing to this young man's father and then forward it to Rheims to cover expenses. This he attempted to do, but meeting Francis Goare, a tailor, and a cousin to both families, he identified himself and stated his business. Thinking that Goare had gone to fetch the money, he waited. But Goare returned not with the money but with the local Watch. Hence Laurence Johnson was arrested, convicted on account of his priesthood, and executed at Tyburn on 30 May, 1582. He died with three other priests - Thomas Cottam, William Filbie and Luke Kirby. All were offered their lives if they would take the Oath of Supremacy which they all resisted. Stonor says that Queen Elizabeth was dancing when their death warrants were brought to her for signature. After pausing to sign, she continued dancing. (24)

The English Jezebel

The years 1582 to 1588 were truly frightful ones for many of the English Catholics. In 1582 there were eleven executions, in 1583 there were four, in 1584 nine, in 1586 fifteen and in 1588 the unprecedented number of thirty-two. In 1587 there had been eight but that included Mary Queen of Scots who was beheaded in Fotheringay Castle on 8 February, because Elizabeth feared an uprising with Mary figuring as her rival. This provoked tremendous condemnation, Pope Sixtus V denouncing Elizabeth as "the English Jezebel" even though he retained a high regard for her statesmanship.

Catholic Europe was indignant, Philip of Spain sent his Armada to attempt an armed intervention. Everyone knows that it was a complete failure though few are aware that Drake's second-in-command in that redoubtable victory was the Catholic Lord Howard of Effingham. On the whole, the English Catholics gave Spain no support whatsoever. Perhaps the old Marian priest, James Stones captured near Ormskirk in 1585 "complete with Catholic books and massing equipment" spoke for them when he said "I wish Elizabeth Nestor's years but her Majesty's laws spiritual are not established according to God's laws."

But the backlash against Catholics following the defeat of the Spanish Armada was such as not even the tranquillity of Little Crosby woods could withstand. For the next hundred years the Blundells of Crosby, while never actually boasting a martyr for the Faith, produced a succession of sturdy confessors whom neither Oliver Cromwell, William of Orange nor the gates of hell itself would prevail against. (25)

The Blundells go to Gaol

On 11 June, 1590, Lord Derby sent a party of his men to Little Crosby to question Richard Blundell and search his house. It was led by young Richard Molyneux from Sefton, grandson of Sir Richard Molyneux who had signed Laurence Vaux's oath of loyalty to the Pope twenty-four years before.

Richard Blundell's son and heir, William Blundell (1560-1638) who had been educated at Douai and had married Emilia Norris, daughter of yet another staunch old Lancashire recusant, Sir William Norris, of Speke Hall, wrote an account of the events of that day and the next few years. They can best be told in his own words:

"The 11th June the Rt. Hon. Henry, Earl of Derby, sent certain of his men to search the house of Richard Blundell of Little Crosby for matters belonging to Catholic religion, where they apprehended and took away with them to his honour's house (New Park, Lathom) one Mr. Woodroffe, a seminary priest, and the said Richard Blundell and me, William Blundell, son of the said Richard; and the day next following we were severally examined by the Earl; and on the thirteenth day of the said month we were all sent to be imprisoned in Chester Castle. About the fifth or sixth day of August next following, we were all by the Earl's men fetched from Chester and brought to Knowsley, one of his honour's houses, where we were (as also my mother and John Carr, my father's man) severally examined by Chaderton, the Bishop of Chester, who was joined in commission with the Earl to examine us upon interrogations by the Lords of the Council. And the day following, the priest, my father and I were sent prisoner to Lancaster (where we found prisoners there before us Mr. Henry Lathom of Mossborough and Mr. Richard Worthington of Blainscough, committed for their conscience) where also my father and I remained for the most part until the 10th March, 1592, on which day my said father changed this life for a better. Within about a fortnight after, I had a licence, obtained from the Rt. Hon. the Earl of Derby, to come to Crosby for only one month; and then returned to Lancaster again, whence, about Michaelmas ensuing or somewhat before, I was again dismissed by his honour's warrant.

But on the 20th or 21st November next after, I was again approached by John Nutter, parson of Sefton, and divers others assisting him, and my wife also was taken, and both of us first were carried to the Parsonage of Sefton and there stayed all night, whence on the morning we were brought to my Lord's house, the New Park, before the Earl, the Bishop Chaderton and Mr. Wade, one of the Clerks of the Council, where my wife was dismissed and I, with others, sent to London with two pursuivants. And on 8th December (being the feast of the Conception of Our Blessed Lady) I, with Henry Lathom of Mossborough, was by the aforesaid Mr. William Wade brought before Dr Whitgift, Archbishop of Canterbury, at his house, Croydon in Surrey, where we were adjudged to prison, Mr. Lathom to the Fleet and I to the Gatehouse of Westminster, where I remained prisoner till the 12th July, 1595, then was set at liberty upon bonds to appear and come within twenty days after warning given, since which time I was never imprisoned.

And so coming home with my wife, who had come up to London with her brother, Edward Norris, and he returning after a few days, she stayed in prison with me till my said delivery, which was six or eight weeks. And after, we lived at Crosby until the 27th May, 1598, at which time my house was searched by Sir Richard Molyneux and John Nutter, parson of Sefton, when I escaping, my wife was taken for her conscience and carried first to Sefton, and examined, and returned home that night upon bonds or promise of my father Norris (Edward Norris of Speke) - as I think - to appear at Chester before the Bishop such a day. Accordingly the last of the same month, she, together with other Catholics.....were committed to prison in the Castle of Chester.

And within little more than a month after, some man (but I never knew who it was) caused the old indictment for entertaining a seminary priest, which had been in the year 1590, aforesaid, to be prosecuted against me. Whereupon proclamation was made according to their custom at the County Courts at Lancaster that I should come in and appear, which I not doing was condemned of felony by the Coroner. After this condemnation I tarried secretly at country houses some three quarters of a year. And in the meanwhile, my wife getting out of prison in Chester Castle upon bonds for her appearance again, she and I, for fear of being apprehended, went first to Wrexham in Wales, where our brother Banastre dwelt; and thence after a good while my wife (being great with child) returned into Lancashire to Speke, and I rode to Wem, where my brother Banastre had another dwellinghouse. And thence to London to get a pardon, where, sending home my horses, I, with my man Peter Stock, stayed there about five weeks. And without getting a pardon I came into Staffordshire, changing my name, whither my wife came to me, and there we stayed about two years at six several places until the Queen's death; when coming home, I soon after obtained from King James a free and large pardon, which cost me in all about 40 or 50 shillings." (26)

Many theories have been formulated and projected as to why English Catholicism survived the onslaught of the Reformation. I close this chapter with one of the best, expressed in the prayer composed by William Blundell himself during those years of hardship. It is spiritual strength, a virtue that can so easily evade the compilers of statistics or the experts in semantics.

Jesu, by thy grace sweeten so our crosses
That we may never faint, fall, or cast them down;
Make us well content to sustain our losses,
Whereby thou dost work us a blissful crown;
Yet, good Lord Jesus, lay no more on us
Than thou givest strength to bear,
Bear we see we must, yet in thee we trust
To bear all with gladsome cheer;
Give us what thou biddest, and bid what thou pleasest,
Fully we ourselves resign;
In thy Church protect us, when we sin correct us -
Not our own we are but thine.

25

CHAPTER 1

Kings, Queens and Countryfolk

Notes

(1) P. Hughes, *The Reformation in England* 3 vols. (London 1954) Vol 1, p281.

(2) *Catholic Encyclopedia* 15 vols. (New York 1907) Vol 15, pp685-687.

(3) Hughes Vol 1, p295.

(4) Hughes Vol 1, p315.

(5) Hughes Vol 1, p319.

(6) F.O. Blundell, *Old Catholic Lancashire* 3 vols. (London 1925 - 1941) Vol 1, pp32-48.

(7) F.O. Blundell Vol 1.

(8) C.L. Lamb, *The Story of Crosby* (Crosby 1936) p29.

(9) J. Bossy, *The English Catholic Community 1570 - 1850* (London 1975) p150.

(10) F. Tyrer, *The Blundell of Crosby Family - A Short Illustrated History* (Crosby 1960) p16.

(11) Tyrer.

(12) W.R. Brownlow, *A Short History of The Catholic Church in England* (London 1897) pp 405-408.

(13) Chetham Vol.12, New Series 1887, Crosby Records.

(14) Hughes Vol 3, pp33-35.

(15) J.S. Leatherbarrow, 'The Lancashire Elizabethan Recusants' in Chetham Vol. 110, New Series 1947.

(16) C. Haigh, *Reformation and Resistance in Tudor Lancashire* (Cambridge 1974); J.A. Hilton, *Catholic Lancashire* (Chichester 1994) p7.

(17) D. Mathew, *Catholicism in England 1535 - 1935* (London 1938) pp35-36.

(18) Haigh.

(19) Leatherbarrow.

(20) Leatherbarrow.

(21) Haigh.

(22) J.L. Whitfield, 'William Allen 1532 - 1594' in Clergy Review Vol 3, (1932) pp 441 - 454.

(23) Hughes Vol. 3, p344

(24) J.A. Myerscough, *A Procession of Lancashire Martyrs and Confessors* (Glasgow 1958); R.J. Stonor *A Catholic Sanctuary in the Chilterns* (London 1951) p254

(25) Haigh; A.E. McKilliam, *A Chronicle of the Popes from St. Peter to Pius X* (London 1912).

(26) F. Tyrer, 'The Recusant Blundells of Crosby' in *North West Catholic History*, Vol 7, (1980).

CHAPTER 2

Buried Treasure

"Among the Turks and Saracens is greater liberty of Religion. The Moors and infidels restrain not Christian rites with such severity"

Ralph Buckland
Dialogue of Comfort, 1605.

It must be borne in mind that from the earliest days of Queen Elizabeth's reign to the Jacobite risings in the 18th century some Catholics never lost hope that somehow events might give them another Catholic monarch. There were others willing to swear allegiance to the temporal sovereignty of any who would grant them freedom of conscience. Sometimes the interests of both sides collided as in 1603 when the latter group desired to present to the Queen a petition known as the Protest of Allegiance, promising civil obedience but begging religious liberty. To the other side it was unthinkable to even acknowledge what they considered to be the personification of evil. The Queen died before it could be presented. (1)

The Stuarts

Hopes rose when her successor, James I, son of the ill-fated Mary Queen of Scots was proclaimed. But there were to be some bitter disappointments because when he discovered that in one year alone recusancy fines fetched him £371,000 he decided he literally could not afford to give relief. So, after including one hundred and sixty Catholics in his accession honours, marrying a Catholic and wishing none of his subjects any ill, King James permitted religious persecution to take its course.

Anyone observing the era of the Stuart kings must inevitably enquire why there were so many apparent contradictions. They all married Catholic queens and allowed Mass and other elaborate ceremonial at Court while priests were being hung drawn and quartered for ministering to ordinary people. When civil war came, the King had no more faithful supporters than the Catholics while those of his own religion put him to death. In 1622, when according to law no Catholic priest had a right to be on English soil at all, James I in London argued about doctrine with the Jesuit, John Percy, pending the conversion of a court favourite. Then his successor, Charles I, when not for the first time fleeing the state of penury, conceived the idea of practically offering discount to Catholics who paid their fines fully and promptly. When the same King attempted to act as supreme governor of the Church of England, an office that Parliament had sanctioned at least twice, it was Parliament that took the greatest offence. Even in Crosby the man responsible for preserving the King's Peace was father of the man who signed the King's death warrant. If this well-nigh inexplicable mixture can be digested we shall be free to follow the events of the 17th century as they affected the people of Little Crosby. Animosity from outside there was in plenty but as long as the Blundell family paid the fines, which had taken on the form of a license to be a Catholic, Catholicism remained, tormented but intact. (2)

Family Relationships

From 1592 to 1638 the manor of Little Crosby was held by William Blundell, he who gave such a vivid account of his father's demise and won for himself the epithet "The Recusant." Of solid piety, he was a hard-working, country-loving squire who enjoyed visiting his friends, going to markets and fairs, and writing verse or prose. He was to write a detailed account of the Penal Laws and of their effect on himself and his family. He gave it the title QUID ME PERSEQUERIS (Why am I persecuted) and it was a work that his grandson often read. His brother Richard became a priest and like Laurence Johnson before, became chaplain to the Houghtons at Park Hall. His daughter Margaret became Sister Winifrede at Louvain.

Despite having, upon payment of forty shillings, received a pardon from King James I, William Blundell still had to contend with an awful lot of legal wrangling over part-sequestration of his lands and the problems created by new, and often unsatisfactory tenants. He had received part of his education at Douai, where the register states he was of gentle birth and had previously been educated with such care as to have had no experience of schism or heresy.

His wife, the former Emilia Norris was equally staunch. Her father and later her brother owned the historic Speke Hall, where priests always lived or received hospitality. This brother, William Norris, figured in a much-publicised case in which he was accused of asserting that a certain Justice of the Peace was "no gentleman" and striking him with the flat of his sword because he had made enquiries among the churchwardens about Norris's church attendance. For this he was fined one thousand pounds.

Nicholas Blundell, son of William and Emelia, was either born in prison while his mother was suffering for the Faith or while she was on bail accordingly. He married Jane Bradshaigh of Haigh near Wigan, but as he died in 1631, predeceasing his father by seven years, it was their son William, known as "The Cavalier", who was to succeed to the estate and hold it for sixty years.

The early 17th century witnessed something of a rise in the standing of the gentry, chiefly because of shrewd business methods and good estate management. This contrasted noticeably with the position of the aristocracy whose extravagance and ostentation damaged their economy and angered the Puritans at one and the same time.

In or about 1609, the date is uncertain, William the Recusant built the present Crosby Hall. The priest's chamber was high up under the roof, a site favoured in several places as letters of the period, offering compliments to "the gentleman at the top of the house" disclose. (3)

Laws Enforced

Since about 1170 the villages of Little Crosby, Thornton, Aintree and Litherland formed the parish of Sefton. Its church of St. Helen, rebuilt in the splendid Perpendicular style about 1500 would have been the scene of their baptisms, weddings and funerals, their Sunday Mass and their Lenten confession. It stood close to the ancestral home of the Molyneux family who held the manor from the time of William the Conqueror; from 1462 to 1557 five successive rectors of Sefton were members of the Molyneux family. Sometimes, like their successors after the Reformation they lived elsewhere and employed curates to do the everyday work. Tithes had to be paid by all the villagers and these sometimes took the form of sheaves, lambs, wool or eggs. In Elizabeth's reign, Richard Blundell had complained that the parson forbade him to pray in his chapel and seized a fat ox. This is a reference to the Blundell Chapel in Sefton Church.

As the impact of the laws of 1559 became obvious, altars, statues, crucifixes and vestments were discarded and burned. All the stained glass in Sefton church was destroyed but that may have been done later. Congregations broke into factions. Firstly there were those who accepted the changes without complaint. Secondly were the Church Papists who fulfilled the letter of the law but made it plain that it was no more than that. Old depositions refer to conservatives who seem to have been people who attended but expressed reservations about what was happening and never received communion. The recusants of course never went near the place until they were carried there to be buried.

Little Crosby Village Cross 1824

From Little Crosby along the route to Sefton church was a series of medieval stone crosses, most of them can be identified today if only partially. They are near Hightown Station, in the village, Virgins Lane and Broom's Cross at Thornton. These were funeral crosses where coffins being carried to burial could be set down while the bearers rested and prayers for the faithful departed were said. As has been seen the Sefton rectors of the 16th century acted against Catholics only sporadically, even slothfully. But in 1602 there arrived one Gregory Turner who for thirty years, supported by Edward Moore of Bank Hall, Bootle, a local Justice of the Peace and one of the few west Lancashire gentry who was not a Catholic, prosecuted with vigour not only the prosperous but also the poor. They did not hesitate to seize animals in lieu of fines and Turner even resorted to forbidding the burial of the dead. (4)

Regrettably an event that happened miles away, an event that the impartial historian Tupling says no Lancashire Catholic was ever suspected of supporting, provoked another outburst of anti-Catholic activity. The story of the Gunpowder plot has practically passed into folklore. If there was a plot no one has ever produced a convincing explanation. Some say a few exasperated Catholics whose minds were living in Tudor days when plots real or imagined were always being exposed, acted reprehensibly. Some say it was a protest against King James the First's refusal to consider the plight of his Catholic subjects. Some say it was Government propaganda aimed at a still considerable religious opposition. But with fifty persons involved at a time when there were nine thousand Catholics in Lancashire alone, it could hardly be called a Catholic plot. But as at the time of the Armada, hostile agents exploited the situation for all it was worth and Catholics everywhere were made to suffer.

Some years later William Blundell wrote: "A bitter storm of persecution extended its fury into these parts to the bodies of all devoted Catholics. The Church in all places denied them burial. Some were laid in the fields, some in gardens, others in highways. As it chanced one of these, I have heard it credibly reported, being laid in common land her corpse pulled out by the hogs and used accordingly."

Time might have been exceedingly slow in producing its proverbial healing qualities but William the Recusant moved to rectify the problems confronting all the devoted Catholics who sought proper burial of their loved ones. (5)

The Harkirk

Within the demesne wall of Crosby Hall lay a plot of land known as the Harkirk, a word of Saxon origin meaning something like old grey church. There was in fact some belief that a place of worship had once existed there. William made this area available to Catholics, now denied the right to bury their dead in the State churchyards, for use as a cemetery.

Out of all the interest that recusancy at Little Crosby has ever generated, the story of the Harkirk is unrivalled. Up to 1951 there were twenty known published references ranging from the prestigious and many-volumed Victoria History of Lancashire and the transactions of learned societies, to the threepenny Catholic Truth

Society pamphlet Catholic Landmarks around Liverpool. Between October 1950 and October 1951 the site was excavated so there need be no conflict between pious tradition and archaeological evidence.

The names of those buried at the Harkirk were preserved and modest memorials of local stone, lettered somewhat amateurishly by a hand not unlike that of William Blundell, were placed there. Between 1611 and 1743, one hundred and five laity and twenty-six clergy were buried, often at dead of night. The laity were sometimes brought from as far as Liverpool and once from the Wirral peninsula. The clergy, mostly from west Lancashire, included William's great-grandson Thomas Blundell, priest of the Society of Jesus. (See Appendix 1).

Of course The Recusant was not allowed to get away unpunished, but retribution came about eighteen years later, after riotous behaviour in the village and will be described under that heading. (6)

Many years later, in the year 1889, another Blundell of Crosby caused a small memorial chapel to be erected at the Harkirk and the names of the dead to be inscribed on its interior wall. In 1995 the Harkirk was the basis of a fifty-four page dissertation by Professor Daniel Woolf of Dalhousie University, Halifax, Nova Scotia.

It should also be made clear that after a few years the ban on Catholic burials at Sefton church was less rigidly imposed and several Blundells were buried there as were two priests who had served the Molyneux family and the district.

The Treasure

The first burial, that of William Mathewson of the Moorhouses, Little Crosby, took place on 7 April, 1611 presumably under cover of darkness. The following morning, Thomas Ryse, the fourteen year old son of John Ryse, a tenant farmer was taking the Blundell cattle to graze in a nearby field. Near the Harkirk he caught a glint in the sunlight and found there a number of silver coins, unlike any he had ever seen. He took one to Crosby Hall to show to the other servants and to Edward Denton who although able to read could not identify the coin. William Blundell himself later wrote of how from his own antiquarian interest and with the help of books from his library, particularly the 1594 edition of Camden's Britannia, he suspected (wrongly) it to have formed part of an issue of Peter's Pence which was the tribute paid from old Catholic England to the Holy See of Rome. Together with Nicholas his son, Denton the secretary, and with Thomas Ryse he went to the place of the find. More coins were found and on a further visit, accompanied by his wife and his mother, still more were discovered. This "unexpected gift from Heaven" as he put it, or the reward for his generosity as others saw it, amounted to a minor hoard of four score silver coins "none bigger than a groat" and several other fragments. Later scholars have been as impressed by the books of reference that William possessed at the time, as with the find itself. It was to be identified as having been left by the Danes within a few years of their retreat to Northumbria in the year 910. It consisted of items from the reigns of Alfred the Great, Edward the Elder and King Canute, as well as others bearing "strange and unknown inscriptions."

After arranging the coins in the form of a cross, William had a copperplate engraving made, a reproduction of which appeared in the 1887 Chetham edition Crosby Records. There, with Gothic horror it is related that burial places were often sites of hidden treasure and offered an unidentified verse to support the claim. It may sound more Victorian than Anglo-Saxon but it is well worth the quote:

> Trust not would his experience say,
>
> Captain or comrade with your prey,
>
> But seek some charnel, when at full,
>
> The moon gilds skeleton and skull,
>
> There dig your tomb your precious heap,
>
> And bid the dead your treasure keep.

Whatever else, we can be certain that it was disturbing the ground to make the graves at the Harkirk that unearthed the silver. Here also is seen William Blundell's subtlety. He never employed workers to dig for treasure because he knew the law, an ancient one that dated from the time of Edward the Confessor, which held that treasure collected on his own land by his own family differed from that which was dug up and could be claimed by the Crown. He also knew that gold could be claimed in the same way, but silver could be divided between the finder and some charitable cause if it was found in a church or cemetery. This is exactly what he did. Some of the coins, at least thirty-five of them were kept for drawing and engraving. The others were melted and made into a silver chalice which was stolen sometime in the 19th century, and a pyx, that is a snuffbox-like container used to transport the Blessed Sacrament to the sick, which remains at St. Mary's Little Crosby and inscribed "This was made of silver found in the burial place. W.Bl." Thirty years later at the time of the civil war the other coins were taken into Wales, never to be heard of again. (7)

Riotous Behaviour

The Council of Trent said it is possible to be responsible for another's sin in nine different ways, and provocation is one of them. Between 1612 and 1629 the inhabitants of Little Crosby and district were subjected to enough harassment as to constitute provocation by any standard. The County Record Office possesses

The Harkirk Chapel from a painting by Col. Nicholas Blundell

33

all the depositions written by those who carried out the actions in the name of the law. To describe them all in detail would be exceedingly tedious for writer and reader alike, so similar are they all. But they have been painstakingly transcribed from their quaint old English by the late Frank Tyrer. They leave the distinct impression of Church and State conspiring to make life as difficult as possible for a community whose only aspiration was to live in peace. (8)

The Privy Council complained that the Blundells of Crosby and the Irelands of Lydiate were the most notorious Papists of that end of Lancashire. Land, animals or even wearing apparel was to be seized if the recusancy fines were in arrears. But friendly Justices of the Peace would warn of impending raids, and goods and animals could then be removed to safe custody elsewhere. Sir Edward Moore of Bank Hall, three miles ride across Seaforth Sands, was a Justice of the Peace but not a friendly one. With Parson Turner of Sefton he employed as bailiffs Richard Hardman, William Cowper, Henry Thompson and Peter Brooke, occasionally three others. They were Puritans from Bolton or Bolton-in-the-Moors as it was then called.

On 24 March, 1612 Lord Derby gave orders to parsons, vicars, curates and church-wardens that all recusants should be disarmed and the weapons stored at their own expense. He also wished to receive the names of all recusants and non-communicants. About the same time Ambrose Astell, who seems to have been imposed on William Blundell as a tenant by way of some legal compromise, was making difficulties. In 1613 he threatened to bring William and Emilia Blundell and six others, Richard Narrone, Thomas Burghe, William Harrison, Thomas Marrowe, Thomas Rothwell and James Harvie before the infamous court of the Star Chamber. From his own erudition William Blundell was able to arrange for James Harvie alone to travel to London and deal with the matter. It must have been settled amicably because on Harvie's return William wrote "Proceedings proved counterfeit and so ended. Blessed be God for all his mercies and good-ness for evermore, Amen."

In 1622 Recusancy charges were made against the aforementioned Thomas Burghe who was then eighty years old. He was ordered to appear at Lancaster, an impos-sible journey for a man of his age. Fortunately at nearby Ince Blundell there lived a Lincolns Inn lawyer, Robert Blundell, who was able to draw up a statement that produced an acceptable result. But then Edward Rice, yeoman of Little Crosby, was ordered to appear at Lancaster on 26 August, 1622. As he was on bail on a surety of £20 and neither he nor his surety did appear, whether recalcitrant or for a genuine reason we shall never know, the bailiffs were ordered to act, and on 7 May, 1624 they tried to do so. (9)

Some years earlier in an attempt to bring peace in such situations, Pope Clement VIII had written "Exhibit all becoming attachment and reverence and obedience to rulers. Commit no act which will disturb the public peace or offend princes or magistrates or bring religion into hatred or suspicion." But having given warning that they intended neither to give up their faith nor their goods, the Little Crosby folk retaliated. Seven bailiffs came and seized two oxen and a nag belonging to the accused Edward Rice. But, so we are told, they did not hold them long because sixty men and women armed with pitchforks, cudgels and other weapons, attacked, rescued the animals and wounded the bailiff named William Cowper. (10)

Next time, half a hundred persons or thereabouts being able persons and well-weaponed with pitchforks, longstaffs, muckrakes, one spear or pike of war and other weapons prevented any confiscation at all. And even shouted intemperate words!

Next, great commotion and one bailiff sore wounded. All riotous persons were Popish recusants mostly tenants, farmers, servants or retainers of William Blundell Esquire, the said William Blundell and Emilia his wife did look out from their casements and incourage the said persons to make rescue." Later the local miller joined in the affray and the evangelical purity of the bailiff's men was further offended at the spectacle of one man who stood at a corner and who did utter foul words.

Two months later they all had to appear before Sir Edward Moore and Parson Turner at Ormskirk where two of the villagers, Richard Brough and Richard Royce again shouted and used disrespectful words. But after a stern reprimand they were all released.

In September 1624, goods and chattels of William Blundell to the value of £86.13.4d were ordered to be seized on 11 October. Once again the bailiffs came to Little Crosby where servants saw their approach and herded the cattle to safer pastures. Then armed as before "the bailiff's men were sorely wounded and sixteen persons armed with pitchforks warned them to keep away or they would get more."

This was so serious that Sir Ralph Assheton, High Sheriff of Lancashire complained to the Privy Council not only about the behaviour of the rioters but also about William Blundell's demeanour. On 30 May, 1625, the Privy Council empowered one Oswald Moseley, Robert Fazakerley and others to meet at Wigan and hear what answer William Blundell and Emilia his wife had about affairs at Little Crosby, and answer the Privy Council on parchment by Michaelmas.

On 10 August, 1626 by using enormous force, Sir Edward Moore and his son, Colonel John Moore, seized thirty-five beasts, two horses and twenty-nine swine valued at £158 in all. These were sold for £130 to Thomas Hill, maltmaker of Duxbury. There was still a lot of resistance. Cudgels and improper language rent the air, seven of the Sheriff's officers sustained broken heads but fourteen of the rioters were injured. The outcome was that William Blundell was fined £2,000 but on appeal, the new king, Charles I, short of money already, settled for £250 in cash.

It was after these disturbances that on 7 September, 1626, the Harkirk was investigated by Roger Kenion and Andrew Lever who came from Whalley. A few days later "the High Sheriff with thirty men pulled down the wall, knocked the gravestones to pieces, carried away the crosses with much derision, all done with the sound of a trumpet, coming and going in great pomp." Burials did continue and the one gravestone left unscathed in the attack, that of a priest who had died in 1624, may still be seen, preserved in the Harkirk memorial chapel. During one of the foregoing enquiries, all from the village denied that they had been required to contribute to the cost of laying out the graveyard. (11)

Pilgrimage to Holywell

Across the Mersey from Liverpool and across the Dee from Neston stands Holywell, whose fame is conveyed in its name. Since the 7th century, when St. Winefride was killed for her virginity, a spring of water reputed to possess miraculous properties has attracted the faithful. The reformers did their best to discredit the shrine and warned householders and innkeepers to beware of recusants but pilgrims continued to flock there. On St. Winefride's day, 3 November, 1629 an estimated crowd of fifteen hundred attended which included many priests and at least thirteen of the Lancashire gentry; Sir Thomas Gerard, Sir William Norris, Sir Cuthbert Clifton, Sir John Talbot, Preston of Furness, Anderton of Clayton, Anderton of Ford, Gerard of Ince, Bradshaigh of Haigh, Harrington of Huyton, Blundell of Crosby, Scarisbrick of Scarisbrick and Lathom of Mossborough. A note made later by William Blundell had a very topical overtone. He wrote "Mr. Arrowsmith's clothes and the knife that cut him were in the possession of Sir Cuthbert Clifton." A timely reference to the Jesuit martyr Edmund Arrowsmith, executed at Lancaster the year before. (12)

Nunc Dimittis

The year 1631 was very sad for William Blundell the Recusant, as both his devoted wife Emilia and their only son Nicholas, only just thirty years of age, died in June of that year. Legal proceedings brought more adversity and recusancy demands placed almost two thirds of his land into sequestration. Later, at the age of seventy-five, he was called to attend a special hearing at York, so grave was the deterioration in the situation. But he was able to evade the hazardous journey and the impending ruin. Fortunately, William possessed a masterly understanding of the penal laws and he had some excellent Protestant friends. The system he had developed was to "give" his money to these friends in time of prosperity then in time of urgency they would "lend" it to him. Obviously such an arrangement required great trust and no little amount of risk, but it worked. Years later it was said that in London it was as dangerous to attend Mass in 1770 as it was in 1570 but by then the Blundells were playing bowls with priests, parsons and Protestants, mainly due to William's sterling integrity. When he died on 2 July, 1638, he was able "by God's goodness" as he put it, to leave his grandson and successor well provided for. He also left £20 and twelve months salary to the esteemed Edward Denton and a years wages to all his servants. (13)

Civil War

William Blundell was eighteen years old when he succeeded his grandfather in 1638. He liked bright clothes, horses, dogs, hawks, dancing and writing plays. As he did not speak French it is presumed he had not received the continental education traditional among such families. But he had visited Ireland and was acquainted with the Earl of Strafford. At fifteen years of age he had

The Pyx made from coins found at the Harkirk

married Anne Haggerston of an old Northumberland Catholic family and whose two brothers were to be killed defending the Royalist cause in the approaching war. When war broke out in 1642, William Blundell was commissioned as a captain to raise a hundred dragoons. The document, dated 22 December, 1642, required him to defend "His Majesty's royal person, the two houses of Parliament, the Protestant religion, the law of the land and the liberty and prosperity of the subject." He earned for himself the title "the Cavalier" a description that adhered just as firmly as that of "the Recusant" typified his renowned grandfather. (14)

The causes of the war are quite remarkable. In 1531 when Henry VIII declared himself supreme in Church and State, Parliament fearful of the executioner, assented. In 1559 when Elizabeth upheld the claim, fearful of the Pope, Parliament assented again. But when in 1625 the new King, Charles I, declared that he had received these rights from Almighty God, Parliament, fearful of neither executioner nor Pope, took issue and decided to teach him otherwise. It voted that custom's duties, which was money the King needed to live, instead of being granted for a lifetime, as was formerly the case, should be allowed for one year only and then reviewed. Having such a high opinion of himself, the King did not take kindly to being put in his place, and time had many more things to add to their grievances.

The Parliamentarians, with Sir Edward Coke whose knowledge of common law was unique and John Pym whose understanding of political manoeuvring was unrivalled, on their side, tended to see every wish of the King as a challenge to their principles and instead of addressing legislation spent a lot of the time searching out and asserting ancient rights. Most deadly of all perhaps, in religious division they saw an indispensable weapon of war.

When in 1559 Queen Elizabeth deprived all the Catholic bishops of their sees, there was, even then a body of extreme Protestant opinion that thought they should not be replaced. However, they were replaced and the new ones were charged to remove this Puritanical element from the Church of England. They attempted to do so, not by actual persecution but by petty restriction and censure. As a group the Puritans gained in strength and often fell foul of the law by criticising, and sometimes denying Elizabeth's position as supreme governor of the Church. At Bury St. Edmunds on 4 June, 1583, John Coppin and Elias Thacker were hanged for refusing to acknowledge the royal supremacy. Here was a stark contrast with the position of the Catholic martyrs who resisted any change at all provided by Protestants who considered changes had gone nowhere near far enough.

The Puritan ideal flourished but suffered alienation, and by the early 17th century boatloads were sailing to America to create godly settlements as far removed as possible from the state of corruption that they believed the Anglican Church to be. Some Puritans who remained would have continued as Anglicans if permitted to dispense with certain practices such as the use of the surplice or the sign of the cross in baptism. But royal disdain and episcopal intimidation forced them into a camp of militant sectarianism. They resented the very idea of cakes and ale, maygames, rushbearings, piping and dancing, bear baiting, Jesuits, seminary priests, popish feasts and singing hymns.

Matters were not helped when Archbishop Laud of Canterbury reminded the King, when on one of his not infrequent expeditions to raise money, of the old law of 1559 that fined someone a shilling for Sunday non-attendance at their local Anglican church. It was applied vigorously and resisted by the Puritans almost fanatically, as they endured croppings of hair, brandings and the pillory. Laud had said patronisingly they might think what they like but they must conform in public worship. They did indeed think what they liked and literally finding an axe to grind they succeeded in getting Laud beheaded. When they took up arms in support of Parliament it was already a body that contained a good many of them. That Parliament pressed upon the King a list of impossible demands: bishops no more to vote in the House of Lords, no more bishops ever to be appointed, all the King's ministers to be approved by Parliament, abolition of the Book of Common Prayer, control of the Church and the Army. (15)

War becoming inevitable, Oliver Cromwell led the Parliamentarians. He was a great nephew of the man who had devised the dissolution of the monasteries a century before. His name became synonymous with ruthlessness and he infused into the Irish psyche a hatred of the English that time itself has not yet eradicated. It has been estimated that 3.7% of the population died as a result of the war, a death rate higher than that of the first World War. Lancashire suffered considerably. There was an heroic siege at Lathom House near Ormskirk, battles at Whalley and Preston, Prince Rupert captured Liverpool for the Royalists though at enormous cost of life. William Blundell advanced on Lancaster in company of the Earl of Derby on 18 March, 1643. There William received the musket shot in the thigh that excluded him from further war service and gained him the nickname Halt Will.

As the Parliamentarians improved their positions daily so the prospects of the Blundells declined, indeed their fortunes were never so low as in those middle years of the 17th century. On 30 January, 1649, the King was beheaded in Whitehall. One of his judges had been Colonel John Moore (d. 1656) of Bank Hall, son of Sir Edward Moore who had taken such aggressive measures against the Crosby Catholics before being suddenly struck dead in a Liverpool street in 1632. Colonel Moore was also one of the signatories of the King's death warrant.

For the next eleven years the Government of England meant the Protectorship of Cromwell during which William Blundell came close to ruin. For the remainder of his life brief moments of optimism and hope were to be inundated by years of near despair. But Catholicism was a way of life at Little Crosby and though great were to be the trials, greater still was to be the resistance. (16)

A Cavalier's Note Book

The Parliamentarians called their defeated opponents delinquents. If they happened to be Catholics as well, they were called malignant delinquents. Being of this latter sort, the years of Cromwellian rule meant imprisonment four times for William Blundell, not just for a few days at a time but lengthy terms like the entire winter of 1656. This was in Liverpool Castle which in his opinion was the worst of them all, a filthy place where pthisis (tuberculosis) was rife. While incarcerated there he received news of the birth of his ninth child, a daughter.

Tax demands and legal arguments over recusancy arrears were such as to occupy a massive roll, twenty feet in length, still to be seen at the County Record Office, Preston. These, in short, amounted to William possessing nothing and being indebted to the sum of £81. How he extricated himself we cannot precisely explain although something he wrote at the time offers a little more than a clue. "Many persons have money which they desire to put out for lawful interest but they are wholly ignorant of the means to do it .... others know not where to find it." We have seen previously that his knowledge of business and law was extremely astute. This, together with the support of good friends meant that what had been achieved before was to be achieved again, but it was going to demand unceasing effort and well-nigh indestructible moral fibre.

William made the aforementioned remarks in a hand written book that he commenced in 1659. In 1880 it was edited and published entitled *A Cavalier's Note*

Book - Notes, Anecdotes and Observations. While not a diary in the real sense, it gives a picture of his world as he saw it. We know from it that he had a fascination for church towers and steeples and liked to climb them. He observed that the average age of the people living in the twenty houses of Little Crosby was sixty years. He joked about the time he said to a poor woman he would give her sixpence for her children and she replied that she would not sell them. He was amused by the story of the Scottish laird who had his Sabbath alcohol seized - legally - by officers who drank it on the spot, so repeated the offence substituting poison which nearly killed them. He mentions a terrible wreck off Formby, in September, 1673, which involved a loss of eighty lives. But generally speaking it portrays a society full of unbelievable contradiction and injustice, which he summarises as "Catholics deny the oath yet keep their allegiance to the King. Others take the oath and fail in allegiance."(17)

New Reign - Old Laws

In 1658 about the time of the death of Oliver Cromwell, William went abroad mainly to escort two of his daughters to the Benedictine's convent at Ghent (Gant, as he invariably wrote it) where they intended to become nuns. Continuing to travel, he arrived at Breda in the Netherlands where the Stuarts were living in exile. He got close enough to see the Dukes of Gloucester and York playing ninepins, with their brother the future King Charles II watching. Eventually, in May, 1660 William returned to England on the same ship as Charles who had been invited to reclaim the throne. Full of gladness and with promises of toleration for all, he had accepted. But after bells had rung and the bonfires had blazed and the musicians had performed and the people had danced - all such activities having been forbidden for eleven years - things took a decidedly ominous turn.

Having learned nothing from the immediate past, Charles allowed himself to be persuaded that religious differences were not things to be tolerated. The Church of England, it was purported, alone should supply spiritual sustenance. This, redolent perhaps of the Duke of Buckingham's answer to a question what was his religion: "I have not the faith to be a Presbyterian or the good works to be a Papist so I am Church of England." Anyhow a new law decreed that none may hold any public office who did not receive communion in the National Church. Two thousand former Puritans, renamed Dissenters, were driven out, the Rector of Sefton among them, but while legislated against the Dissenters were never quite as disliked as the Catholic recusants. Despite the proven loyalty of the latter it was put about that their first duty was to a foreign prince - the Pope - and Justices were advised to be very severe against them. As usual there were to be special exceptions. The fact that Charles II tried to induce the Pope to create Philip Howard, son of the

Earl of Arundel, a Cardinal was one, and eventually successful. But a tragic end awaited William Blundell's friend Richard Langhorne who had received special permission to continue practising law in London. (18)

We are now dealing with a time of much injustice, made worse in so far as the interpretation of the law varied from place to place. In some quarters recusants who had supported the Royalist cause were refused a hearing because of their religion while Roundheads were confirmed in tenancies they had obtained because of theirs. Little Crosby once more became a target of frequent disturbance. Baptisms not performed by the parson at Sefton were still chargeable at four shillings a time, tithes were exacted and recusancy arrears constantly demanded. As it was impossible for the poor agricultural labourers whose income never approached twenty pounds a year to pay the recusancy fine of that amount a month, a succession of visitations, threats and renewed demands was always in progress.

A new local tax added insult to injury by compelling people to pay the expenses of being summoned to pay in the first place. William Blundell questioned the propriety of this but such was his treatment that on a future occasion he did not bother to prosecute poachers, so disenchanted was he with the system.

When William wrote to influential Protestant friends in London imploring them to search for means of relief, it was not only freedom of worship that he had in mind, but some release from the financial fetters that were cramping his entire community. Promises and soothing words he received in plenty, but no respite. When in 1665 the City of London was devastated by the bubonic plague, he in one of the few bitter comments that can ever be attributed to him, said it was a punishment sent by God. (19)

Mercifully there were some moments of pleasure. When William was in prison in Liverpool Castle in 1656 he met a young man named Richard Butler who was heir of the Earl of Mountgarret. In 1661 Richard married William's daughter Emilia, and later in 1679 succeeded to the Earldom. At Michaelmas 1663, the Provincial of the Jesuits, Fr. Edward Courtenay accompanied by William's uncle, Fr. Peter Bradshaigh, visited Lancashire where it was claimed they had 2500 penitents. Clearly their stay at Little Crosby inspired many a depressed soul. In 1664 William went on pilgrimage to Holywell. His companion was Laurence Ireland of Lydiate who died in 1673, the last male survivor of that faithful old family. (20)

A friendly Protestant magistrate, John Entwistle, would give warning when house searches were imminent. Richard Langhorne who was William's legal adviser in London thought times were so dangerous that placing the Little Crosby estate into sympathetic Protestant hands ought to be seriously considered. Once again William was fortunate in possessing in John Chorley, Mayor of

Liverpool, a friend willing and able to transact all that was necessary. It proved to be a satisfactory arrangement until tensions eased somewhat. William himself was inclined to think that none but a mad man would instigate all the action that it was possible to take against Catholics. Regrettably a mad man did.

Before explaining the madness, or sheer malevolence of Titus Oates, we might look at a list of Little Crosby recusants compiled for the Government in 1671. It includes most of the adult population of the village. (20)

William Blundell, Esquire	Richard David
Anne, his wife	Elizabeth, his wife
William Blundell, gentleman	Ellen Worrall, widow
John Aynesworth	Isabell Mercer, widow
William Harrison, labourer	John Fisher, labourer
John Barton, husbandman	Thomas Tickle, labourer
Ralph Barton, husbandman	Ellen, his wife
Margrett Rothwell, widow	William Weddow
Thomas Rothwell, husbandman	Thomas Mercer, husbandman
Ellen, his wife	Ellen, his wife
John Marrell, husbandman	Elizabeth Ridding
Cecilia, his wife	George Ridding, webster
Ellen David, widow	Brian Lea, husbandman
Margaret Rice, widow	William Bushell, labourer
John Haworth, husbandman	John Blanchard, husbandman
Anne, his wife	Robert Thompson, husbandman
Hugh Reynold, yeoman	Margrett, his wife
William Stock, husbandman	Brian Richardson, husbandman
William Arnold	John Johnson, yeoman
Richard Arnold, his son	John Williamson, husbandman
James Rice, husbandman	John Rydeing, husbandman
Jane, his wife	Nicholas Blundell, taylor
Margaret Sephton, widow	Margery, his wife

Thomas Arnold, taylor

Thomas Farrer, husbandman

James Farrer, his son

Elizabeth Rice, widow

Laurence Blundell, husbandman

Robert Moorcroft, husbandman

Catherine, his wife

The Popish Plot

Titus Oates was one of humanity's misfits. Expelled from school, unsuccessful at university, ejected from the Protestant ministry because of immoral conduct, a social outcast. It dawned upon him that to discredit the papists in a spectacular manner would possibly restore something of his tarnished reputation.

To understand the phobia that then existed among ordinary people it must be appreciated that King Charles II had no legitimate children to succeed him. He had several illegitimate ones but that was of no consequence and to his credit he did not abandon his barren queen. But the heir presumptive, James Duke of York, was not merely a nominal Catholic but a fervently committed one. In 1677 James entertained all the priests of the London district in his apartments in Whitehall Palace and petitioned the Pope to send England a Catholic bishop once again. (21)

Precisely what the population feared from Catholicism is doubtful if any one of them could have defined. Some may have suspected foreign alliances at a time when English nationalism was strong, some perhaps thought a curb might be applied to the pursuit of immorality in which so many of the aristocracy excelled. Some possibly saw their positions of influence and power being removed and handed to their rivals. Some dreaded being compelled to partake in acts of idolatry like the queen in her palace, even that the fires of Smithfield might be rekindled. Whatever their view of Catholicism the one way in which they all stood united was in the fact that they didn't want it. It was a situation crying out to be exploited and the previously insignificant Oates seized his opportunity. Having prepared himself well by visiting the Jesuit College at St. Omers and the English College at Lisbon, feigning friendship and receiving hospitality, he took action. The outcome of this action brought panic generally, excruciating martyrdom to a number of innocent Catholics, and profound grief to William Blundell whose own son escaped only narrowly.

In association with Dr. Israel Tonge of London, a fanatical anti-Catholic pulpiteer, on 26 October, 1678 Oates placed before the authorities details of an imaginary plot to murder the King, put James on the throne, overthrow the Government and replace it with a council of Jesuits, and then carry out a general massacre of Protestants. Some of the details were so fantastic that even the King himself queried them but when the man to whom the report had been delivered was found stabbed to death a month later, that fact also was attributed to the plotters. (22)

Oates very artfully interspersed his accusations between genuine names and real places to such a degree that any reasonable person would have experienced difficulty in separating fact from fallacy. When the contents were released among a hostile and ill-informed people the reactions were positively horrific. In all twenty-six people, eighteen priests and eight lay men were executed solely for their religion across an area that spread from London to Chester in the north, and Cardiff and Hereford in the West. Innumerable others were imprisoned some of them left languishing for years.

William Blundell's friend, Richard Langhorne, was among the first to be arrested, known as an eminent lawyer who had been granted special exemption to remain in practice for the previous fifteen years. He was taken to Newgate Prison and after a farce of a trial in which two witnesses swore he was nowhere near the house that his accuser said was the centre of the plot, because he would not take the oath denying the Pope's primacy, he was sentenced to death. Sentence was deferred for a time in which it was hoped his professional integrity might merit a reprieve. From the condemned cell he wrote a most courageous letter saying "I have not only a pardon, but also great advantages as to preferments and estates offered unto me.........but Blessed be God who by his grace hath preserved me from yielding to these temptations." Richard suffered at Tyburn on 14 July, 1679 and was declared Venerable by Pope Leo XIII on 29, December 1886. (23)

Oates' treachery almost penetrated the Blundell's family circle. William and Anne had two sons who were priests and they will receive more attention in the next chapter. But the eldest son, Fr. Nicholas Blundell, S.J., somehow attracted the attention of Oates. Nicholas had spent the greater part of his life as a priest teaching philosophy to Jesuits in training at St. Omers. He had never worked on the English Mission. But for a period of months covering the years 1678-1679 he was resident in London attending to the business and finances of the Society. According to Oates, Nicholas Blundell was chaplain to Newgate Prison where it was his duty to convert the condemned prisoners and catechise children with seditious doctrine. He was also accused of plotting to destroy London by fire from Westminster to Wapping and to take leave of his friends by saying "Be of good courage, Protestantism is on its last legs." Even in this deposition Oates used the names Nicholas and Richard Blundell haphazardly. He then contrived an arrest to bring him before the Privy Council but the man he had said was Nicholas Blundell was in fact, Fr. Peter Alexius Caryll, O.S.B. In Council the Earl of Shaftesbury who definitely had no popish sympathies was quite taken aback and asked "Since when has Caryll the Benedictine become Blundell the Jesuit?" Caryll, who was a grandson of Lord Petre and had on occasions been one of the Queen's chaplains and therefore known at Court, replied "Since Mr. Oates on his oath has been pleased to endow me with that personality." Meanwhile Nicholas had returned to St. Omers. (24)

Further restrictions were imposed on ordinary Catholics. They were forbidden to keep inns or alehouses, or to travel more than five miles from their homes. At Ormskirk Catholic books were burned in the market place while people produced papers certifying that they had taken the oaths. At Simonswood, Croxteth and Toxteth there was no constable to administer the oath but at Little Crosby the constable, Thomas Coppul, had not taken it himself. For this he was fined two pounds. Over the Christmas period of 1678-1679 the Hall and all the cottages at Little Crosby were thoroughly searched and every person over sixteen years of age was ordered to attend Sefton church on 9 January to take the Oath of Allegiance and Supremacy. Not one of them went which meant further court appearances at Ormskirk or Wigan, and severe reprimands for seventy-five people, William and Anne Blundell included.

Demands started to come from certain quarters that all the known Catholic gentry, Henry Blundell of Ince Blundell and William Blundell of Crosby among them, should be deported. The idea was soon discarded because expense alone made any such plan totally unrealistic. But William, now sixty years old, weary and dispirited, decided to depart of his own accord. Some say he had considered relinquishing the estate and not returning at all.

As he was forbidden to travel more than five miles he wrote for permission to go abroad. When asked for what reason, he was perfectly honest and replied that it was to escape the penal laws. He was told that he may go but under no circumstances would he be allowed to return. He made another attempt to obtain the correct permit, offering "five or six pounds if granted." It never was granted but he went, taking with him his grandson, Edmund Butler, who was placed in the college at St. Omers. How did he get to France? We do not know. Possibly in disguise, possibly smuggled out in a small boat. Perhaps through a distant port where he would not be recognised. Did he even go by a secret route known only to Catholics at the time. We cannot say, but after placing all his business interests in the hands of John Chorley, go he did. (25)

As William had five daughters who were nuns in various continental convents it is probable that he visited them. However, no sooner had he set foot in France and took up residence at Laflech than the news reached him that his son Nicholas, priest of the Society of Jesus, had died at the early age of forty. William remained abroad until 1682 by which time life at home was much less perilous. Passing through London on his journey north he saw the men building the new St. Paul's Cathedral. A few years later the whole country knew that Titus Oates had been found out as the liar he really was and that the pension and grace-and-favour residence that a grateful people had hastily voted him had been even more hastily taken away.

The Blundells go to Gaol again

Early in 1685 King Charles II after asking his closest associates not to let Nellie, his favourite mistress, starve, turning Catholic on his death bed and apologising for taking so long over dying, did so. His brother was proclaimed as James II so after an interval of a hundred and fifty years England had a Catholic King again. The new King was convinced that by forever compromising with Parliament his father had lost his kingdom, so he took immediate steps to let it be seen he had no similar inhibitions. He gave notice that the Coronation ceremony would not be taking place within the Anglican Communion Service and it did not. But he did revive the ancient custom of washing the feet of twelve of his subjects on Holy Thursday, the last English monarch ever to do so.

James proceeded to fill various royal and academic appointments with Catholics while ponderously telling the Anglican bishops that as long as he could be assured of their loyalty they had nothing to fear.

His close friends and the Pope's representative at his court advised prudence and not to attempt too much too quickly. But whether we ascribe the reason of his tolerance as expressed in the Declaration of Indulgence (which offered religious freedom to all) to being enlightenment ahead of its time, or of his wilfulness as being that of a despot only interested in getting his own way, the fact remains that to be impeded was to James absolutely abhorrent.

In Lancashire 55 per cent of Crown appointments went to Catholics and other Dissenters with the commensurate number of Anglicans ousted. The Earl of Derby was replaced as Lord Lieutenant by William Molyneux, a recusant and William Blundell junior of Crosby was among twenty-seven newly created Catholic magistrates. Doubtless the old Cavalier himself would have received something by way of recognition but age and infirmity was beginning to declare itself. It is said that James, by his high-handed and insensitive dealings with the Anglican ascendancy did more to expose Catholics to contempt than either the Civil War or the exploits of Titus Oates. The Dissenters were never won over by his liberality and after a reign of a little less than four years he was compelled to abdicate. (26)

King James II left Catholics at least one lasting monument of his zeal, namely bishops. England had known no Catholic bishop since Elizabethan times. It is true that between 1623 and 1631 some attempt had been made to provide an episcopal presence. But one had died within a year of appointment and the other fled, as much the victim of the wrath of his co-religionists as of his enemies. In 1685 James secured from the Pope the appointment of a Vicar Apostolic, that is a titular bishop permitted to govern by emergency regulations as it were. John Leyburne was made Vicar Apostolic of England on 9 September, 1685. He undertook a general visitation of the Kingdom, administering Confirmation in places where it had been unknown for more than a century. At Croxteth Hall, which was the nearest he came to Crosby, in excess of a thousand people received that almost forgotten sacrament from him. In 1688 the number of Vicars Apostolic was increased to four who were assigned districts called the London, the Midland, the Northern and the Western. Little Crosby being in the Northern district was to welcome a number of future Vicars Apostolic because that system of Church government remained until the reign of Queen Victoria and after the building of the present St. Mary's. (27)

Following the flight of James II it was Parliament which determined policies and laws more and more and the personalities and predilections of monarchs mattered far less than in the past. The crown was offered to James's daughter Mary, whose husband William of Orange insisted upon reigning jointly as William III. Catholics expected very little by way of kindness from him. One of the next laws was to make it impossible for a Catholic ever to be King of Great Britain again, but James by raising an army in Ireland still hoped to regain his kingdom. This led to William Blundell's fifth term of imprisonment on account of his religion. In 1689 he was held at Manchester for seven weeks in company with several other prominent Catholics including Charles Towneley of Burnley of whom William said "His company would make life pleasant anywhere." It transpired that they had been imprisoned to prevent them from joining James in Ireland, or assisting others to do so. After that William seldom left Little Crosby, tethered as he put it, by the five mile chain. Some of their horses were seized on a number of occasions, at least once without any proper authorisation, but other than that times were relatively peaceful, until 1694.

At half past five on the morning of Monday 30 July, 1694, three law officers and two informers arrived at Crosby Hall with the intention of arresting William Blundell who was then seventy-five years of age. As he was lame through arthritis, a consequence of his old war-wound, they took William his thirty-seven year old son instead. They also took two pistols, two swords, a fowling piece, seven horses and two saddles. Even in those partisan times there were people who questioned the legality of taking a son into custody in place of a father, but it made no difference.

In company with a number of other prominent Catholics, members of the Houses of Clifton, Dicconson, Gerard, Langton, Molyneux, Stanley and Walmesley included, William was put on trial in Manchester charged with plotting to restore King James II to the throne. In point of fact there was, in certain places but not at Crosby, sympathy with what was to be called Jacobitism, that is militant loyalty to the House of Stuart, but there was no proof at that time. The arrests were based on prejudice rather than evidence and the whole event was so clumsily processed that the jury aquitted them all. It was not until 1927 that the real evidence emerged with the deciphering of secretly coded papers.

Seen in perspective Catholics were neither alone in their preference for the Stuarts nor in taking positive action to improve their conditions. While James II was still

King, Henry Compton, Protestant Bishop of London committed the treasonable act of signing a letter inviting William of Orange to take the throne. When that was accomplished Archbishop Sancroft of Canterbury refused to crown William and went into a state of ostracism because he recognised the law of heredity.

Death of the Cavalier

On 24 May, 1698 the old Cavalier, William Blundell, sixty years Lord of the Manor of Little Crosby, died. He was buried, without objection, in the Blundell Chapel at Sefton church. We cannot do better than allow part of his own testament to be the last words on his long life filled as it was with great sorrow and an even greater fortitude. He wrote "No rebel ever in the Town of Little Crosby. Great grand-father died in jayle (sic) for having a priest taken in his house A.D. 1591. Grandfather five years imprisoned, most virtuous and learned. Remember the burial place we have had of our kindred who are, partly dead partly living, no fewer than sixty-seven persons of both sexes who have been either Religious or priests, whereof five of my own children, three of my Father's children, eight uncles and eight aunts and eleven cozens. My own family consisted of fourteen children of whom four died in infancy. Of the other ten, three sons and seven daughters, two sons became priests and five daughters became nuns."

His son, Fr. Thomas Blundell, S.J. was at that time a priest in Lancashire, probably with the Cliftons at Lytham. Although there is no proof that he offered his father's funeral Mass secretly at Little Crosby, in such a family it is inconceivable that it was otherwise. (28)

For the last few years of his life the Cavalier was described as a tabler, that is a guest, in the house of his son and heir who was also named William Blundell. Partially for legal purposes, partly because of his father's infirmity, William had taken on the responsibility for household and estate. Although not destined for longevity, having been a convicted recusant and imprisoned, he was a typical Blundell. He had also asserted his right to examine the Sefton churchwarden's accounts to satisfy himself that recusant fines were being correctly entered at a period when such monies were often at the root of dishonesty and abuse.

On 27 July, 1702, William was taken suddenly ill and on 2 August, at half-past ten in the morning, just as Mass was ending, he died at the age of forty-five. Three days later his body was taken to Sefton and buried in the same grave as his mother, Anne. William was married to Mary Eyre, daughter of Rowland and Gertrude Eyre of Hassop, Derbyshire. The Eyres were yet another old recusant family, somewhat migratory, but with property in Oxfordshire, Derbyshire and Yorkshire. After her husband's death Mary became a nun in the Benedictine convent at Ghent where she had the uncommon experience of being a postulant in the house of which her own daughter was Abbess.

Finally, a prayer from a manuscript belonging to the Blundell family, attributed to Abraham Cowley of Sefton in 1694. (29)

> For the few hours of life allotted me
>
> give me Great God but bread and liberty;
>
> I'll beg no more, if more thou'rt pleased to give
>
> I'll thankfully that overplus receive;
>
> if beyond that no more be freely sent
>
> I'll thank for this and go away content.

Buried Treasure

Notes

(1) W.M. Brady, *Annals of The Catholic Hierarchy* (London 1877) pp70-71.

(2) R.G. Dottie, 'John Crosse of Liverpool and Recusancy in Early 17th Century Lancashire' in *Recusant History* Vol. 20, May 1990 pp31-47; Stonor, F. Tyrer, *Recusancy of The Blundell Family and Inhabitants of Little Crosby* ms. Crosby Library C949.72 Cro.; T.H. Watkins, 'King James I Meets John Percy S.J.' in *Recusant History* Vol. 19, October 1988 pp146-154.

(3) Tyrer.

(4) Tyrer.

(5) Tyrer.

(6) Tyrer; D.R. Woolf, *The Ancestral and The Antiquarian: Little Crosby and the Horizons of Early Modern Historical Culture*. ms. Crosby Hall Archives.

(7) Chetham Vol. 12, New Series 1887, Crosby Records; Woolf.

(8) Tyrer.

(9) Tyrer.

(10) Tyrer.

(11) Tyrer.

(12) Catholic Record Society Vol. 3, 1906 p108.

(13) Tyrer.

(14) T.E. Gibson (ed.), *A Cavaliers Note Book* (London 1880).

(15) W.S. Churchill, *A History of the English-Speaking Peoples* 4 Vols. (London 1956) Vol 2, pp134-144; P. Hughes, *The Reformation in England* 3 Vols. (London 1954) Vol 3, p182; G.H. Tupling, 'Causes of the Civil War in Lancashire' in *Transactions of Lancashire and Cheshire Antiquarian Society* Vol. 65, 1955 pp1-32.

(16) *A Cavaliers Note Book*.

(17) *A Cavaliers Note Book*.

(18) J. Bossey, *The English Catholic Community* 1570 - 1850 (London 1975) pp68-70; Tyrer.

(19) *A Cavaliers Note Book*.

(20) Tyrer.

(21) Jane Lane, *Titus Oates* (London 1949).

(22) Jane Lane, *Titus Oates* (London 1949).

(23) *A Cavaliers Note Book*; R. Challoner, *Memoirs of Missionary Priests* (London 1924) pp 538-541.

(24) H.N. Birt, *Obit Book of the English Benedictines* 1600 - 1912 (Edinburgh 1913) p57; Tyrer.

(25) Tyrer.

(26) *A Cavaliers Note Book*.

(27) B. Hemphill, *The Early Vicars Apostolic of England* (London 1954).

(28) *A Cavaliers Note Book*; E. Carpenter, *Cantuar - the Archbishops in their Office* (London 1988) pp213-222.

(29) P. Doyle, 'An Episcopal Historian' in *North West Catholic History* Vol. XV 1988 p9; F. Tyrer, *The Great Diurnal of Nicholas Blundell* 3 Vols. (Lancashire and Cheshire Record Society 1968) Vol 1.

At Home and Abroad

"What is wanted is a man of wit and conversation, one that can preach well and is willing to take pains amongst the poor Catholics, of which we have a great many, one that is of good humour and will be easily contented with tolerable good fare."

Nicholas Blundell
to the Jesuit Provincial, 1707.

The holy sacrifice of the Mass is at the heart of all Catholic worship. The belief that after the consecration Christ becomes truly present, body, blood, soul and divinity and that the sacrifice of the altar is one with the sacrifice of the cross, has prevailed throughout the Church in all times and places. But of all the severances instigated by the reformers of the 16th century, their aversion to this belief was unsurpassed in its detestation. Altar stones were used as doorsteps and cowshed floors, sacred vessels were denigrated into tableware, laws made it a capital offence to celebrate or assist at Mass, clerics trod the sacred host underfoot and well into the 20th century monarchs were required on oath, not merely to reject Catholicism generally but to recognise that Mass was a blasphemy and deceit.

It is not easy to explain this irascible attitude. Luther himself is supposed to have said that scripture and antiquity was strong in favour of the doctrine but he was tempted to deny it in order to give Popery a slap in the face. Two hundred years before, St. Thomas Aquinas in his great *Summa Theologica* had anticipated and answered two hundred and eighty possible objections, many of which never even occurred to the reformers. Then about 1840, safely guarded from danger by a gap of another two centuries, the Anglican divines of the Oxford Movement almost found delight in reviving the word mass and all its implications.

Danger

Obviously to attend Mass in the 16th and 17th centuries involved great risk as well as a lot of inconvenience. In London it may have been possible to go into the chapel of an Embassy of one of the Catholic states. But whether that or to the barns, inns, garrets and manor houses of the provinces, there was always the danger of exposure. The activities of government spies, the malice of the common informer, the dubious friend tempted by the reward of ten pounds or most bitter of all, the evidence of the apostate Catholic were all causes for anxiety. On 26 October, 1623 there was a most appalling tragedy in the Blackfriars district of London when out of a congregation of three hundred people, eighty including the priest were killed instantly or trampled to death when the floor of their secret location collapsed. (1)

Little Crosby is Steadfast

The Blundells of Crosby were by no means alone in welcoming the holy sacrifice into their home. Several houses, Hazlewood in the West Riding, Stonor in the Chilterns, Battle in Sussex - its surrounding countryside known as Little Rome - were equally accommodating. Probably every county could point out a place of refuge. But the Blundells were undoubtedly among the first to take the risk and while other places may have flourished and faded, Little Crosby has remained steadfast in its unbroken fervour.

But the Mass requires the presence of a priest and priests require formation and direction. Of those who served at Little Crosby, often enduring long hours of solitude and living always under threat of dire penalties, what is known of them and their times must be of interest to us. (2)

Names

We have seen that Cardinal Allen's seminary priests did not reach England until 1574 but that Richard Blundell was in trouble for harbouring priests in 1566. So, as the Benedictines did not return before 1603 and the Jesuits only arrived in 1580, those first secret Masses at Little Crosby must have been offered by old Marian priests, those ordained in or before the reign of Queen Mary. We can discount the romantic notion that foreign priests roamed hereabouts because neither Cardinal Pole nor Queen Mary would entertain such an idea, even when put forward by Ignatius of Loyola himself.

Although of somewhat homespun quality and in no way as competent in debate as the young men of Allen's regime, the old Marian clergy were popular with the people because philosophically they were willing to live life as it then was and not as how they would have it be. This approach was to be roundly condemned by the Jesuits to whom anything not positively combating heresy was not only wasteful but sinful. Yet even their undeniable successes moved one sober old soul to remark that it seemed more for the love of Jesuits than for the love of Jesus.

The first names found at Little Crosby possibly relate to the same person, John Peel or John Pycke, reputedly officiating about 1568. But the records of the seminaries and of the religious orders cannot help us to identify him. In a masterly survey of the entire period Christopher Haigh says he was from outside the county and came attracted by the prospect of harvesting many recusants. James Darwen certainly ministered here. Formerly curate of Sefton, he had conformed to the Church of England but was reconciled by John Musson, a priest who had been in the household of Edmund Bonner, the last Catholic Bishop of London. Very different is the case with Robert Woodruff, the Mr. Woodroffe of William Blundell's graphic account of his father's arrest. He was born at Banktop in the parish of Burnley in 1552. After study at Douai and Rome he was ordained on 13 December, 1581 by Thomas Goldwell, the exiled Bishop of St. Asaph. Bishop Goldwell, deprived of his See by Queen Elizabeth in 1559 was, with Richard Watson of Lincoln, the last surviving member of the old hierarchy of England that could trace its origins from St. Augustine. After spending some time at his mother's house in Burnley, Fr. Woodruff went to Mr. Blundell's at Little Crosby where he was captured on 11 June, 1590 and convicted at Lancaster. He was imprisoned there and later at Wisbech and Framlingham, these latter places being special houses of detention for priests. In January, 1601 he was banished from the kingdom and returned to Douai.

Different again is the story of a priest who came in 1592, but the heroism of a Campion was not to be found just anywhere. The old Crosby records call him George Dingley but his real name was James Younger and he was born in 1563, at Eaglescliffe, Co. Durham. He left Durham Grammar School ostensibly for Cambridge but in reality for a continental seminary. He was ordained in Rome on 1 May, 1587 in the Lateran basilica. It is stated that he taught in the English College and preached the annual St. Stephen's day sermon in the presence of the Pope. In 1589 he was sent to England to beg for funds where he made contacts in the Lincolns Inn area of London and lodged at the White Swan, Holborn. He was arrested and on his own admission he gave away information in order to obtain his release. Then he travelled north but while at Crosby he informed against James Gardiner, a priest who lived at Ince Blundell disguised as a schoolmaster. By 1593, Younger, or Dingley or Leighton or Christopher - he is known to have used all these names - was back at Douai and was later sent to Lisbon where, past failings pardoned, he excelled as a teacher. But he was never permitted to visit England again.

About the same time James Forth, a seminary priest (not Forde a Jesuit as is sometimes stated) was ministering here. It was a very bleak period when even the oil used in the sacrament of extreme unction had to be smuggled from France or Ireland. Fr. Forth was a son of Alexander Forth of "Swindley" (Hindley?) sent back to England after his ordination at Rheims in 1584. He sometimes used the name Bank as an alias. In 1586 he was in the house of Thomas Birchall of Billinge and the Douai Diary records that he was with the Blundells of Crosby sometime before 1593. We know nothing of his subsequent career or death. (3)

Catholicism Transplanted

Early in the 17th century, about the time that William the Recusant was preparing for the Harkirk, it could have been said that a portion of English Catholicism had experienced something of a transplant. From the imposition of the repugnant oaths in 1559 to the furore over the Gunpowder conspiracy in 1605, every fresh wave of anti-Catholicism resulted in a few more joining the little colonies of exiles for conscience in Brussels, Madrid, Paris or Rome. At Louvain academics lived in two houses called Oxford and Cambridge.

By the reign of James I, Catholics had unofficially but definitely been divided into two groups, papists and recusants. The papists were considered the dangerous ones and usually, directly or indirectly, it was they who provided the martyrs. The recusants were looked upon as a lucrative source of income who could be controlled or priced out of existence at will.

Bishops, physicians, philosophers, monks and nuns went abroad in search of peace and found it if only for a time. Nowhere were the English more numerous than at Douai, a town on the river Scarpe, eighteen miles south of Lille. It contained a university and several medieval churches, the Parliament of Flanders met there and in 1568 Cardinal Allen had settled his English College there. However, due to war, or the danger of war, between 1577 and 1584 they had to remove to Rheims but by 1600 they were back at Douai numbering about a hundred and fifty students and their teachers. Douai also contained a monastery of about twenty-five English Benedictine monks and would continue to do so intermittently until 1903. The exiled English Franciscans also had a church and a college with about sixty friars. (4)

The Benedictines

The history of the English Benedictines is long and fascinating and as they were destined to provide eight of the priests who would serve at Little Crosby perhaps a few facts may be given.

The very names of the great English Benedictine foundations have the ring of history about them - Canterbury, Durham, Chester, Tewkesbury, Glastonbury, St. Albans, Rochester, Winchester - and most illustrious of all Westminster, where building or rebuilding never ceased from the Conquest to the Reformation and whose Abbot sat as of right, in the House of Lords.

After dissolution under Henry VIII, Westminster Abbey was restored to the monks by Queen Mary, but in 1559 they were expelled again. By 1606 only one of their number, Fr. Sigebert Buckley, was still alive but he was in prison. Westminster Abbey had never been canonically suppressed by the Holy See so technically all its rights and privileges were vested in this sole survivor. From his prison cell on 21 November, 1607, he affiliated two secular priests, Robert Sadler and Edward Maihew, into this ancient inheritance, thus preserving it from extinction. The deed was witnessed and attested and several years later, after some eloquent advocacy, its validity was accepted by Rome. These new monks joined by others then settled at Dieulouard in Lorraine where, like all the others mentioned in this section, they flourished not as English people absorbed into foreign communities but as communities distinctly English. At Dieulouard under the patronage of St. Laurence, these Westminster monks, consistently reinforced, had a church, cloister, school, farm and brewery. For some reason they held a particular attraction for Lancashire men and there was a period in the 18th century when the entire community came from that western part, between the Mersey and the Lune.

About 1640 the Benedictines also acquired the Abbey of Lambspring in Hanover which they possessed until the time of Napoleon a hundred and sixty years later. Like Dieulouard it attracted many vocations from Lancashire and played an honourable part in supplying priests for the English Mission. (5)

The Nuns

We might admire the degree to which men persevered in their vocations throughout those perilous times, but the women were no less responsive. There were, between the English Reformation and the French Revolution, seventeen exclusively English convents from Belgium to Portugal. There were Benedictines at Brussels, Cambrai, Ghent, Paris, Pontoise and Dunkirk. Three Blundells of Crosby and girls from Ince Blundell and Netherton found their way to these. At Paris the Blue Nuns attracted many widows who resided *en pension.* The Bridgettines from Syon Abbey in Middlesex fled to Lisbon in 1564 and attracted many vocations from the Fylde. The Canonesses of St. Augustine at Louvain attracted Winifrede, daughter of William and Emilia Blundell, who was professed there in 1615. They had a second house at Bruges which Charlotte Mary Blundell of Ince Blundell entered.

There were Canonesses of the Holy Sepulchre at Liege, Canonesses Regular in Paris, Carmelites in Antwerp and Dominicans in Brussels. The Franciscan Observants at Bruges obtained several entrants from west Lancashire, Mary Gilbertson and Helen Molyneux from Ince Blundell and five of the Scarisbricks among them. But none, it would appear, could rival the appeal of the Poor Clares whose convents at Gravelines, Dunkirk and Rouen contained between them fourteen Blundells and five Bradshaighs. (6)

The Society of Jesus

Queen Mary and Cardinal Pole invariably looked upon Catholicism as being synonymous with Benedictine, Carthusian or Dominican spirituality. It can be no more than an interesting speculation as to what might have been the outcome had Mary not died so early, because the culture of the Counter Reformation never really appealed to her. Neither were the Jesuits in any way associated with her policies.

The Society of Jesus, the Jesuits as its members are known, owed its origins to Ignatius of Loyola (1491-1556) and the very climate of the Counter Reformation. Within twenty-five years of its foundation it had 3,500 members and 130 colleges, seminaries and schools. Its missionary activities in India, America and Japan appealed to young adventurous minds but to work for the conversion of England was never part of its early agenda. Indeed many things pointed in the opposite direction, not least the likelihood of martyrdom. Furthermore, it was against its constitutions to live alone, wear disguise, hide their priesthood or consort with people of doubtful moral standards. And their Father General saw no point in sending back to England men who had sacrificed so much to escape from it, for Englishmen had been as plentiful as any in offering themselves. Yet Cardinal Allen, he who founded the seminary at Douai and others in Rome and Valladolid, suggested and argued, inveigled and encouraged until all such obstacles were overcome. After all, scores of his own students had entered the Society!

Though their places of formation varied between Louvain, Liege, Watten or Rome, and from 1593 they kept a school for boys at St. Omers, twenty-six miles south east of Calais, there was a Jesuit mission to England which some have gone so far as to call a Jesuit invasion. The more bitter the persecution the more abundant was the flow of vocations while the Government's response was to make it high treason to withdraw any of the Queen's subjects from the religion established by her authority. To keep a Schoolmaster who did not attend the Anglican church cost his employer a fine of ten pounds a month, the schoolmaster himself going to prison for twelve months.

Meeting fire with fire the Society of Jesus was responsible for the reconciliation of souls innumerable, the future King James II for one, the Earl of Derby on the scaffold at Bolton for another. But the cost was no fewer than twenty-three excruciating martyrdoms.

Sadly the state of Catholicism grew chaotic. There was havoc wrought by spies, apostates and informers, a visible lessening of faith, the sacraments so infrequently available as to be in danger of being thought irrelevant, even dissent among those of the faithful who craved peace at almost any price and those whose defiance practically asked for the rack. Despite this depression an effort was made in Lancashire to organise some missionary activity by taking the boundaries of the old pre-reformation parishes as workable units and distributing them - by what process it is impossible to say - between the Benedictines, Jesuits and Secular clergy. The ancient parish of Sefton was allocated to the Society of Jesus, so for the next hundred and fifty years Little Crosby was to have a Jesuit chaplain. Two of the Cavalier's sons, his brother and one of his grandsons would join the Society and eleven Jesuits would be buried at the Harkirk. (7)

Priests at Little Crosby

During the 17th century the people of Little Crosby and others who lived much further afield were to receive spiritual guidance from five successive priests, three Jesuits and two Seculars. Though I admit a canon lawyer might dispute if the first of them was indeed a Jesuit.

From the middle years of the century Crosby Hall was seldom without a priest in residence. We know the chapel was at the top of the house because in *A Cavalier's Note Book* (p116) William Blundell writes "about seven o'clock we went down to the back porch, where standing still we saw the moon in a full clear orb over the chapel chamber chimney." Henry Foley tells us that the priests lived in close vicinity to the hiding hole "like sparrows at the top of the house, expecting the happy day and the advent of the glory of God, for humanly speaking very little was hoped for." We know a little of their lifestyle as the *Letterae Annuae* (Annual Letters) of the Society are extant from 1635 though we are reminded that cruel circumstances made communications extremely difficult.

Sick calls and pastoral visits were usually undertaken at night, on horseback or on foot, because few others ventured out after dark. All were taught the importance of baptism and how to baptise in a case of necessity and conversions continued to be made but the heavy recusancy fines deterred many more. Miraculous powers were thought to be at work when a priest was called to visit a sick man whose father threatened to invoke the penal laws if the priest came but was immediately stricken by a paralytic seizure; or when a lady offered to teach her Catholic servant to read a Catholic prayerbook and herself received the grace of conversion thereby.

Fr. John Layton was here from 1621 to his premature death in 1624. He had some very famous relations. Son of a Peckham Layton and Dorothy, formerly Gerard, he was born at Gaterlay near Richmond, Yorkshire in 1587 or 1588. His mother's cousin was St. Edmund Arrowsmith S.J., martyred at Lancaster in 1628. Her brother was Fr. John Gerard, a truly great Jesuit who had the incredible experience of escaping from the Tower of London. When John Layton went to the English College in Rome, he stated that he had always been a Catholic, that he was unable to speak of his parent's means on account of the uncertainty of persecution, which meant them constantly migrating between Lancashire, Yorkshire and Buckinghamshire. He also added "What I have gained I owe to the Fathers at St. Omers." He was ordained on 28 October, 1611 and the following year asked to be admitted to the Society of Jesus. He came to Crosby in 1621 with a reputation as a translator to which was added tributes for being an excellent preacher and zealous missioner. He died on 18 February, 1624, aged 36 and is buried at the Harkirk. His gravestone alone escaped desecration in the onslaught of a few years later. The oldest of its type in west Lancashire, it still exists in the Harkirk memorial chapel.

When no priest was in residence at Crosby Hall, Little Crosby was served from Ince Blundell, Croxteth or even Moor Hall near Ormskirk. Then Fr. John Walton arrived and though he did not remain long, he made a great impression. He was born in 1622, in Lancashire, possibly in Sefton parish. Professed as a Jesuit he came to Little Crosby in 1652. He had connections with the University of Louvain and like many of his generation was an ardent controversialist. His argument that no rational person could resist the authority of St. Peter's chair covered a hundred and three pages and was printed in London. He remained until 1656 after which he spent many years at Worcester. He died in London in 1677. William Blundell the Cavalier wrote to him "Your doctrine and your great example would teach us patience if we could imitate as well as remember," and writing from Haggerston Castle to his sister Frances, the same gentleman said "Mr. Walton would be welcome to stay and do nothing."

The next priest, Francis Waldegrave, belonged to a venerable old English family. His grandfather Sir Edward Waldegrave had been a servant of Queen Mary and was one of the first to be punished for defying the new laws of 1559. For supporting a priest and allowing Mass to be celebrated in his house, he was sent to the Tower of London, where being denied medical care when he was ill, he died on 1 September, 1561. His grandson Francis, son of Nicholas and Lucy, formerly Mervin (daughter of a Protestant Dean) was born in Wiltshire in 1626, educated at St. Omers and in Rome and ordained in the Lateran basilica on 25 March, 1651. He entered the Society at Watten in 1655 and was sent to the Lancashire mission. In Rome he was a contemporary of Richard Blundell, the Cavalier's brother who was also studying for the priesthood but died at the age of twenty-two. He was allowed to make his vows as a Jesuit a few days before his death.

Fr. Waldegrave's duties covered an enormous area, taking in places as far away as Culcheth and Bryn as well as nearer ones like Lydiate. The steward at Ince Blundell mentions him in a letter and the Cavalier once wrote to him reminding him that his horse was still at Little Crosby and eating its head off. On another occasion while Fr. Waldegrave was resident at Crosby Hall, William complained that on the feast of the Conception of Our Lady he desired that all should say the Rosary, but Waldegrave was more inclined to play at tables and shovel board. But such was his sensitivity that even the sound of ordinary conversation could be troublesome to him. William on another occasion said "We find much comfort from good Mr. Waldegrave."

Around the time of William's imprisonment in 1689, Fr. Waldegrave suffered many waylayings and insults, especially around Lydiate. It is said that on one occasion a mob set out to kill him but he was saved by his horse taking a wrong turning. He died at Lydiate on 28 November, 1701 and is buried there at St. Catherine's chapel.

A secular priest about whom we know little apart from the fact that he was buried at the Harkirk on 12 October, 1665 is Alexander Barker alias Parr. Son of Richard and Margaret Barker and Lancashire born, he went to Douai in 1621 and later studied with the Oratorians in Paris. He was ordained at Arras on 15 March, 1631 and appointed to the Lancashire mission.

Much better known was Fr. Edward Molyneux, a Secular priest who often supplied. Born about 1640 among the sand dunes two miles to the north of Little Crosby at Alt Grange, a house whose very name was to become synonymous with Catholicism, he studied at Douai. By 1666 he was back among his family. A truly apostolic man, in 1686 he erected what was long known as the Formby masshouse. Two years later it was seized by an anti-Catholic mob who converted it into a tithebarn, but after many more years it reverted to its original purpose and served until the present church of Our Lady of Compassion was opened in 1864.

On 8 May, 1701, Fr. Molyneux's estate being valued at £200, he was outlawed under the new Act of Parliament. A year later, 30 August, 1702 Nicholas Blundell recorded having given to Edward Molyneux, 23 crowns for the clergymen. Fr. Molyneux was killed by a fall from his horse, on 28 April, 1704. He is buried at the Harkirk and it is said that he had been a missioner at Formby for thirty-eight years and had in excess of 800 penitents.

Before leaving the 17th century some mention is called for of the Cavalier's two sons, Nicholas and Thomas Blundell, priests of the Society of Jesus. Nicholas, as we already know, was accused by the dastardly Titus Oates and though he escaped to France died there at the early age of 40. Thomas was born at Little Crosby in 1649 and entered the Society of Jesus at Watten in 1667. Ordained in 1679, he taught philosophy (as did his brother) for eleven years in the continental colleges of the English Province, then in 1690 he became Instructor to the Tertian Fathers (that is those preparing for their final vows) at Ghent. He came to Lancashire in 1692 probably to be chaplain to the Clifton family at Lytham which is where he died on 7 June, 1702. He is buried in the Harkirk. (8)

The 18th Century

This did not begin auspiciously for the Catholic community. The Government, still fearing the Stuarts might instigate trouble and suspicious that Catholics might assist them, took further repressive action. The reward for the capture of a priest was increased from £10 to £100. No Catholic was to inherit an estate which was to pass to the nearest Protestant relative. A fine of £1000 was the penalty for sending children out of the country to be educated with a reward of £100 for anyone who reported them. Other penal laws, of course, remained.

Nicholas Blundell, 1669-1737

All this made hardly any impact at Little Crosby where 33 year old Nicholas Blundell succeeded to his father's estate by the simple expedient of it being given him during the latter's lifetime. As in former times, laws could be circumvented and unjust demands would bring out the best from Protestant neighbours who, in the most literal sense of the words, would hold goods or property "in trust." There was an example of this in 1703 when a token search was made at Crosby Hall and two horses, Jack and Robin, carried off to pay the recusancy fine. The next day the horses were returned, thus showing the willingness of local justices to adhere to the letter of the law while ignoring the consequences.

As Nicholas also had interests in trade between Liverpool and America and a coal mine at Huyton, he was able to face the future with some sense of financial security. He also kept a diary meticulously from 1702 until 1728 which permits us to chart our course with accuracy and ease.

Mass returns to Liverpool

The penal laws placed little restraint if any on the new priest Fr. William Gillibrand, S.J. who was a native of Chorley or thereabouts, and a cousin of Nicholas Blundell. Born 1 October, 1662 and educated at St. Omers, he made his final vows in the Society on 7 September, 1700 having served in London for the previous six years. He came to Little Crosby in 1701. Within two months he had been to Ormskirk fair, seen the Jesuit Provincial at Sefton, gone hare coursing with the parson from Great Crosby and visited Liverpool. This last event is of great significance because Liverpool had known no resident priest since the 16th century. But it had grown tremendously in population and maritime importance. Fr. Gillibrand began to celebrate Mass in the house of Mr. Lancaster, a grocer of North John Street, and later in the house of Thomas Brownbill, a mariner in the same street. In December, 1706 he moved into Mr. Lancaster's and thus was the beginning of St. Mary's, Highfield Street, the mother parish of Catholic Liverpool.

Nicholas Blundell was not at first agreeable to Fr. Gillibrand leaving Little Crosby but excellent relations were maintained and this priest and later his successor in Liverpool, Fr. Francis Mannock, S.J., were often invited to dine at Crosby Hall and indulge in recreation there. The next resident priest at Little Crosby was Fr. Augustine Newdigate Poyntz who arrived on 2 November, 1706, but on 26 January, 1707 he was described in the diary as "very unsatisfactory." On 1 February the Jesuit Provincial was sent a letter of complaint but he was not eager to make another change. On 8 February there was something of a crisis meeting when priests from Ince Blundell and Formby came to discuss the extraordinary matter. Poyntz left quietly on that day, never to be heard of again and obliging the people of Little Crosby to go to Ince Blundell for Mass until the following August. Poyntz apart from reputedly having no social graces and being unable to preach had been expelled from Douai but somehow got himself ordained in Rome, possibly because he was a vociferous anti-Jansenist. There is no evidence of him ever having belonged to the Society of Jesus. His departure prompted Nicholas Blundell to write the letter to the Provincial, quoted partially at the head of this chapter, as to what manner of priest was desirable. On 6 August, 1707, in the person of the Reverend Robert Aldred, S.J. he obtained the very one. (9)

Marriage

For 17 June, 1703 Nicholas, the Diarist entered "I was married to Lord Langdale's daughter." The following day he went fishing! His wife, Frances was the third daughter of Marmaduke Langdale of Heythrop House near Oxford. Marmaduke's father had spent £160,000 of his own money supporting the King in the civil war but received little if any gratitude. The family continued in good works, eventually providing a Yorkshire home for the Canonesses of the Holy Sepulchre of Liege, dispossessed at the time of the French Revolution. Later still they sent to Westminster one of the first Catholic members of parliament after the Act of Emancipation.

Although Fr. Gillibrand travelled with Nicholas to Oxford, a Lisbon educated priest named George Slaughter - presumably the Langdale's chaplain - officiated at the wedding. Four days later Nicholas and Frances paid their respects to Parson Burches and

Part of a page of the Great Diurnal

gave him half a guinea to register their marriage. All was very amicable and a week later the parson, and his wife, called to wish them well before they set off on the eight day journey to Little Crosby. (10)

Recusancy in all of Crosby

Once more, in 1705, a demand was made for all recusants to stand and be counted. Great Crosby, described as having a village green, stocks, three wells, plantations, horse racing and every year on St. Luke's day (18 October), a goose feast at which a fiddler played, contained 138 Catholics. Their names were Alcock, Arnold, Ascroft, Atherton, Blensherd, Bridge, Cartwright, Fisher, Gill, Hump, Hunt, Hutton, Johnson, Kuerden, Larking, Lumbing, Mercer (very many of this name), Nelson, Newhouse, Norris, Rothwell, Sephton, Shepherd, Syar, Tarleton, Thelwell, Thorp, Travers, and Westhead.

Little Crosby numbered 126 viz: Ainsworth, Aldsworth, Blansherd, Blundell (and many unnamed servants), Gilliburn (sic) "a supposed priest", Brianson, Bullun, Davy, Terrec, Gray, Harrison, Howard, Houghton, Jackson, Jump, Mackdanael, Kerfat, Marrell, Molyneux, Ryding, Shepherd, Starkey, Summers, Thelwell, Tickle, Thomson, Warton, Weadal and Wignal.

At Ince Blundell was reported "a good house lately built as is said for ye use of ye priests." Over the years the purpose of this house has caused several misunderstandings as it was known as the college. But it was never one in the sense that students were taught there. More correctly, it was a residence where the Jesuit Provincial sometimes lived and at other times priests rested there or caught up on their reading.

Alt Grange in Little Altcar was another Jesuit house, 100 feet long, 30 feet wide and 40 feet high. In November, 1703 the Vicar Apostolic, Bishop James Smith, confirmed more than a hundred persons there. During the same period he confirmed a hundred and seven at Little Crosby where he received hospitality for seven days. (11)

Ned Howard's Cottage

Nicholas Blundell "the Diarist" was a personality and a man of immense popularity. He enjoyed archery, bowls, coursing, dancing, fishing, shooting and skating. At his table he entertained Alban Butler, author of the *Lives of the Saints*, Parson Wairing of Great Crosby, Parson Letus of Sefton and Parson Stythe, Rector of Liverpool as well most of the Catholic clergy of south Lancashire. When Parson Wairing's son was dying he went to their house to sympathise and when Wairing himself died in 1711 his body was borne to Sefton churchyard in the Blundell's coach. Parsons, priests, gentry and tenants often drank, played cards and bowls together and formed a sixpence a year club to promote discussion and conviviality. The only inharmonious notes were occasionally sounded by Parson Ellison of Formby who had some sort of ongoing squabble with the Catholics of Ince Blundell.

Into this almost idyllic environment on 6 August, 1707, arrived the Reverend Robert Aldred, S.J., who was to remain until his death in 1728. Nicholas described him as a firm friend, companion and adviser who joined all the tenants in sporting and social activities and would gladly lend a hand in the fields. His congregations were fair: 217 at Mass on 9 November,

Ned Howard's Cottage

1707, - 75 at Vespers. Soon after it was decided that Fr. Aldred should leave his room in the Hall and move into Ned Howard's cottage on the western side of the village street and have a proper chapel there. The house is still standing and with a cross above its northern gable, it is the most famous house in Little Crosby. Nicholas took much interest in all of this. He bought a picture from Dr. Lathom of Aintree to be the altar-piece. He helped to fit and secure the altar. He provided a cart to take chairs, forms, curtains, linen and a load of hay. He ordered a tabernacle to be made by William Abbot who lived out among the marshes, and he taught Laurence Blundell, a villager, how to serve Mass. But at the first Mass of all, on 30 July, 1709, the priest was served by Nicholas Blundell himself. All this while the penal laws were there to be invoked!

Sadly, the peace was to be shattered and, as always, the cause of its disruption was created miles and miles away. (12)

The Stuarts Again

In October, 1715 the Stuarts made a not unexpected bid to regain their Kingdoms. There was little hope of success because neither the King of France nor the former High Church Tories showed any signs of interest. In Northumberland the Earl of Derwentwater raised a force and marched on Lancaster where James Edward Stuart was proclaimed as King James III. Liverpool took fright and dug fortifications around the town and molested what Catholics could be found. But the rising was already doomed. As a precaution all the vestments and sacred vessels were hidden at Crosby Hall and several unfriendly visitors (26 of them on one occasion) came and went. Nicholas was compelled to spend six days, on and off, in the hiding-hole and wrote of it humorously as being "a straight place for a fat man." Fr. Aldred was in a very dangerous situation but as there was never a scarcity of friendly welcomes, by constantly keeping on the move he evaded capture and survived the ordeal. However, tidings turned very bitterly against Nicholas, not from action by his Protestant real-friends it must be emphasised, but through informers and mischief-makers from Liverpool, so he decided to go to France, and travelled via London.

Some of the Jacobites were hanged at Preston and others were transported to the West Indies as slaves, but Nicholas was in London on 24 February, 1716, the day Lords Derwentwater and Kenmure were beheaded on Tower Hill for their share in the rebellion. Three days later he attended their solemn Requiem Mass in the chapel of the French Embassy and wrote that several persons of note were present. He remained abroad until September, 1717 by which time it was deemed safe to return. Passing through London he visited Newgate prison to see his neighbour, Mr. Scarisbrick, who with a number of other Lancashire recusants suspected of disloyalty towards King George I was being held captive. He also had the incredible experience of meeting Mr. Robert Blackburne, of Thistleton near Kirkham, imprisoned without trial since the suspected plot of 1694 and destined to remain so until his death in 1747, an injustice unparalleled in British legal history.

The Government reacted to the 1715 uprising by ordering Papists to register their estates. Nicholas Blundell complied and his answer covered six pages of minute script in which every detail of his income is accounted for down to the wages of the humblest servant. In 1723 there was another alarm, a false one as it transpired, that a Stuart uprising was imminent. On that occasion the Anglican Bishop of Rochester Dr. Atterbury was suspected of being sympathetic and arrested. But all the expense of these events was gathered up in a general tax of a hundred thousand pounds to be paid collectively by all known Catholics and non-jurors. On 24 October, 1723, Nicholas Blundell recorded paying his share of £14.7.2d. This is of importance because it was the last legislation specifically against Catholics. It cannot be said that the immediate future was to bring any dramatic improvement, but at least things were not going to get any worse. (13)

West Lane House

It can never be said that to the people at Little Crosby a problem was not seen as an opportunity or that a wrong done to them was not accepted as a cross to be patiently borne. By this inexhaustible blend of patience and hope their every need has always been satisfied. In this spirit, soon after his return from France in 1717, Nicholas Blundell discussed, over a smoked pipe, with Fr. Aldred the desirability, or more probably the necessity, of providing accommodation for the

Rear of West Lane House 1923

faithful superior to the limitations of Ned Howard's cottage. The outcome was that by 13 May, 1720, the property long known as West Lane House had been built. From the lane it resembled nothing but the brick wall of a barn, but on the secluded inner yard were crescent-topped windows, now bricked up but still visible and exhibiting evidence of later adjustment. This was the first building to be erected as a Catholic chapel in England since the Reformation. This distinction is often claimed for the one at Lulworth Castle in Dorset but Little Crosby was sixty years ahead of that. As before, Nicholas served the first Mass there and a week later being Fr. Aldred's birthday they celebrated with a bowl of punch. Those who know the chapel at Dodding Green or who can remember old St. Benet's Netherton, might gain some visual impression of its interior. It was the place where Mass and the sacraments - several of the Vicars Apostolic confirmed here - would be available for Little Crosby until the present St. Mary's was opened in 1847. And it is worth remembering that until 1826, when old SS Peter and Paul was erected, the Catholic people of Great Crosby also came. (14)

Joys and Sorrows

The friendly associations of former years were revived. Four parsons kept company with Nicholas and Fr. Aldred. These were Wairing of Great Crosby (son of the former incumbent), Hindley of Aughton, Acton of Sefton and Brooks of Walton. Wairing was actually present at the Harkirk when Fr. Aldred was buried. The family went to Liverpool to hear Hugh Tootell, better known as the Church historian Charles Dodd, preach. On another occasion they were all entertained by a strolling fiddler and his daughter who danced for them. In August, 1728 the Vicar Apostolic, Bishop Williams confirmed 81 persons in the new chapel and every Christmas day, three Masses were celebrated there.

On 23 February, 1728 Fr. Robert Aldred died after an illness of three weeks. He was born in London on 19 May, 1674 and entered the Society of Jesus in 1697. He came to Little Crosby ten years later and, as is written in the Harkirk register "he was very well loved by Protestants as well as Catholics." Until a successor could be found the faithful walked to Ince Blundell, then Fr. Thomas Lockhart, S.J. did temporary duty. He was born in Hertfordshire in 1672 and entered the Society in 1693. He had served at Cheam in Surrey and Culcheth in Lancashire and after a few weeks at Little Crosby he moved on to the Gerards at Bryn where he died on 2 March, 1744. Fr. James Clifton, S.J. came next and remained until his death twenty-two years later on 27 September, 1750. Lancashire born on 3 April, 1698, he entered the Society on 7 September, 1719. His uncle, William Clifton, S.J. was priest at Formby for thirty years before his death on 29 August, 1749. Both are buried at the Harkirk.

Nicholas Blundell, the Diarist, died on 21 April, 1737. Having no son to succeed him and his elder daughter Mary having predeceased him, the estate passed to his younger daughter, Frances (1706 - 1771). On 31 July, 1733 she married Henry Peppard a Drogheda-born Liverpool merchant. When their son, Nicholas, succeeded on 23 November, 1771, in accordance with the terms of his grandfather's will he reverted to the name Blundell. In 1784 he also married into one of the old English Catholic families when Clementina Tempest became his wife. She was daughter of Sir Stephen Walter Tempest, of Broughton Hall near Skipton, Yorkshire. To their son, William

The Blundell Hatchment, Sefton Church

Joseph Blundell (1786 - 1854) we owe St. Mary's, but before then much else was to happen. (15)

Catholic Politics (1)

In November 1745 the Stuarts made a final bid to regain the throne when Charles Edward Stuart, popularly called Bonnie Prince Charlie, persuaded some, by no means all, of the Scottish clans to rally to the cause. Their immediate victories astonished everyone even themselves. With Edinburgh under control the Prince, against some sound advice, invaded England. This was his downfall because the clans were only really interested in having a Scottish Kingdom and could see no reason to fight over England. On the other hand France, without whose help no lasting success could be achieved, only wanted the Hanoverians out of England and was hardly interested in Scotland at all. So having marched through Carlisle, Preston and Manchester, at Derby they all turned back and in April, 1746 met with an inglorious and final defeat.

In the wake of the rebellion mobs throughout England rampaged and looted. At Preston and Liverpool Catholic chapels were burned. Henry Peppard of Little Crosby was able to give some assistance to Liverpool. As soon as the riot mania had subsided he organised fund-raising to restore the chapel. But Liverpool Corporation, reminding him that this was against the law, refused permission. So the resourceful Peppard said "Very well. But there is nothing to prevent me from building a warehouse and doing with it what I like." So after being cautioned that whatever he did was entirely his responsibility, St. Mary's was built in Lumber Street, near to where Exchange Station is situated today. It did indeed resemble a warehouse with large frontal double-doors and teagle, rope, block and hook suspended above. This sufficed until 1845 when it was replaced with what Bishop Goss used to call the most beautiful church in the diocese.

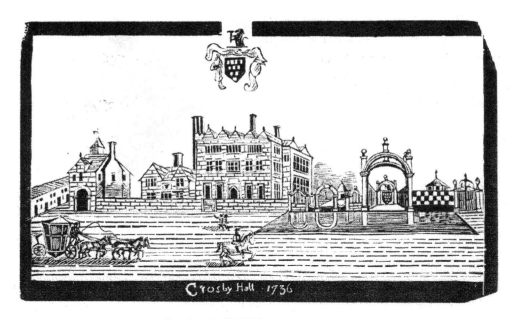

Crosby Hall 1736. from a woodcut

After the defeat of the Stuarts in 1746 and more so when twenty years later Pope Clement XIII refused to recognise the bonnie prince as Charles III, some thought the only prospect for the Church in England was to expire. There was an opposing view. As far back as 1715 one of the Vicars Apostolic - Stonor of the Midland District - had foreseen the futility of forever associating Catholicism with the Stuart cause, and advised against it. After a lot of impassioned debate this idea was to prevail and by the time George III became King in 1760 the Catholic nobility and gentry were busy formulating arguments in support of their appeal for legal relief. There was much hostility to this. Some Protestants said there were no Catholics in England to bother about, others argued they were numerous enough to bring down both Government and Crown. To put such conflicting theories to the test, the House of Lords in 1767 ordered *every* beneficed clergyman in the land to investigate and report on the number of Papists within his parish. These findings, apart from establishing that the total was about sixty thousand, constitute (as far as Lancashire and Cheshire are concerned) a social survey of a minority that is truly outstanding. (16)

The Returns of 1767

At Little Crosby John Sale was quite distinctly registered as a priest. There were 200 other Catholics whose names were Ainsworth, Baines, Bilsbarrow, Blundell, Bridge, Bradshaw, Bond, Budgett, Bullen, Cockshutt, Cross, Davy, Dunsworth,

Farrer, Fisher, Formby, Gerrard, Gilbertson, Gill, Gore, Harrison, Heyes, Hornby, Howard, Hunter, Johnson, Kerfoot, Macdonald, Mercer, Marrow, Morley, Molineux, Newton, Norris, Occleshaw, Orrell, Pinnington, Peppard, Radcliffe, Reynolds, Riding, Rimmer, Shaw, Shepherd, Spencer, Speakman, Taylor, Thelwall, Wainwright, Westhead, and Wharton. Very appropriately Thomas Hunter was a watchmaker, as was Thomas Cockshutt. Otherwise their occupations varied as blacksmith, carpenter, gardener, gentleman, groom, husbandman, miller, pedlar, servant and yeoman: also several spinsters and widows. At Great Crosby there were 154 Catholics, - 71 males and 83 females.

The above-mentioned Fr. John Sale, S.J., was born on 20 October, 1722 at Hopecar near Leigh, where his father had a considerable estate. He entered the Society at Watten on 7 September, 1741 and made his final vows on 2 February, 1759. It is not certain when he arrived at Little Crosby but he was later to serve his native place and then Furness, north Lancashire, where he died on 23 October, 1791. Between the death of Fr. Clifton in 1750 and the arrival of Fr. Sale, Little Crosby had been dependent upon two visiting priests. One, John Talbot (1708 - 1765), was stationed in Liverpool so here we have an example of the daughter mission caring for the mother in time of need. The other, Henry Tatlock (1709 - 1771), a native of Kirkby was chaplain to the Molineux family of Croxteth and provided by them with a fine house of his own near what is now Lower Lane. Mention need be made of Fr. Joseph Blundell, S.J., brother of the Diarist, who died on 27 July, 1759 aged 73 years. He entered the Society in 1703 and served the south Yorkshire - Derbyshire area, living at Spinkhill for many years. Anyone who has read the diary of Nicholas Blundell will be familiar with the name of Walter Thelwell, the long-serving steward. As far back as 1680, when the Cavalier took refuge in France, Walter then a youth accompanied him as servant. He also had two sons who entered the Society: Walter, born at Little Crosby on 15 August, 1723, a laybrother all his life, he died as sacristan at Wardour Castle, Wiltshire at the age of 85. Joseph Thelwell, born 1731, entered the Society in 1750 but died as a novice aged 21. (17)

Catholic Politics (2)

On 14 May, 1778 the Parliament, after a lot of preamble but with very little opposition passed a bill which though grandiosely entitled AN ACT FOR THE RELIEF OF HIS MAJESTY'S SUBJECTS PROFESSING THE POPISH RELIGION just about gave Catholics the right to exist. The penalty of imprisonment for life for bishops, priests and schoolmasters, the reward of £100 for the informer and the prohibition against inheritance were removed. All other disabilities remained, enforceable if not intended to be enforced. Some say it was the emergency to recruit soldiers from among Irish, Scottish and colonial Catholics that was the impetus rather than the representations of Catholics themselves. But doubtless all were grateful if only for an exceedingly small mercy which at least afforded some opportunity to negotiate for more.

Politics of another sort brought about a radical change at Little Crosby. By the middle of the 18th century the Society of Jesus with a world-wide membership of 22,589 religious, 42 provinces, 669 colleges, 61 noviciates and well over 600 missionary projects was both influential and powerful. A little too powerful for some of its critics. In South America the Society had antagonised colonising exploiters through teaching the poor to respect themselves. In Europe it fought the Jansenist heresy bitterly when Jansenism was fashionable and the new Age of Enlightenment viewed heresy hunting with some distaste. So it was not without enemies. But the Papal decree of 16 August, 1773 suppressing the Society and declaring its priests Seculars and its non-priests laymen free to join another order but compelling them to repeat the noviciate if they did so, came as an incomprehensible shock to most people.

Pope Clement XIV had given way to that element in hostile governments that within a generation was to make Europe a battle-ground and within a century attack Rome and the Papacy itself. In England the Vicars Apostolic treated the ex-Jesuits with sympathy. Their Provincial Fr. Thomas More, the last surviving male descendant of the great saint of that name, received the title Grand Vicar and was permitted to continue much as before. But unable to accept new members existing commitments suffered as of necessity. Little Crosby was one of them.

At the time of the suppression of the Society of Jesus, Fr. John Buller was priest at Little Crosby, the last Jesuit to hold this distinction. Born in 1746, he entered the Society in 1768. In or about 1781 he moved to Ince Blundell and remained there until his death on 14 December, 1811. Little is known about his successor but from Bishop Gibson's clergy list of 1784 we know him as J. Barrow and from several items of correspondence with Nicholas Blundell, the Diarist's grandson, we know him to have enjoyed pomposity of language. There were three priests of this name in England at the time but none can be definitely identified as having been at Little Crosby. Whoever he was Nicholas had tried to secure his removal and met with unwillingness and contempt. The priest claimed he had marled a field at his own expense so it would be uneconomic for him to leave. He also proved to be very objectionable on another matter. He threatened to go to law over the possession of West Lane House, which was most improper because had its real purpose become known the consequences for the congregation could have been horrendous. After Nicholas had consulted a lawyer, Mr. Leigh, the priest was induced to leave, but before going he wrote "Remember you are no more than a man; a man perhaps who has no other recommendation to the world than a tolerable fortune of which you have availed yourself if not to distress your dependants, at least to insult the Ministers of God, your superiors in every other line but that of fortune. He that despiseth you despiseth me are the words of our Blessed Saviour........" and there was much more.

To all who know and understand what families like the Blundells had suffered to preserve the Faith the attitude of this priest must seem ludicrously petty. Yet it forms a most appropriate accompaniment to what was happening nationally. There was a good chance that following the Relief Act of 1778 further liberties would be granted. For this the Catholic nobility and gentry had been pressing relentlessly. But the Government had told them that any concessions would be subject to the swearing of an oath. At this the four Vicars Apostolic grew perturbed but when the wording of the oath was revealed they were absolutely condemnatory and made their objections crystal clear. They insisted that they were the true spokesmen for Catholicity, not the laity no matter how articulate was that laity or however much its faith had been put to the test.

The Government's scheme was that Catholics - until 1793 still called Papists - would be divided into two groups, those who would take the oath in which they were described as Protesting Catholic Dissenters and would benefit from the envisaged relief, and those who still refusing would remain being called Papists and therefore get nothing. This controversy set family against family, bishop against people, almost altar against altar. One problem was that after more than two hundred years of intense persecution some of the laity and even a number of the clergy could not see what difference a few words would make, especially as it was asserted they could easily be made capable of orthodox interpretation. But the Vicars Apostolic remained very resolute. They knew well that the whole history of the persecution stemmed from the fact that faithful souls had refused to swear to execrable oaths. We have seen how in the 17th century the Cavalier was edified by people who suffered injustice rather than take oaths they did not believe in, and was scandalised by the actions of those who did. In 1791 an Act of Parliament was passed which due to the tact and goodwill of the Anglican Bishop of St. Davids, Dr. Horsley, required nothing that Catholics might find offensive and allowed them to have public chapels and schools, to send their children to be educated abroad, also many professional openings but not to be judges or Kings Counsellors. They were still ineligible to enter Parliament, to receive a university degree or marry other than by the rites and ceremonies of the Established Church.

But the Vicars Apostolic and the more Roman-minded of their clergy such as John Milner had laid down the policy that would remove the influence of the gentry in the control of missionary activities and place such matters firmly under clerical domination. They had also established their unmistakable claim that they were The Church and not a sect. (18)

In 1786 the Benedictines undertook to supply the priests for Little Crosby, but before introducing Fr. Taylor and what was required of him by the new Relief Act, an event of truly devastating magnitude must be told of.

The French Revolution

Popular image might see the French Revolution as a hungry Parisian mob, attacking the Bastille in 1789, freeing all the prisoners, raising the banner of Liberty, Equality and Fraternity and then doing away with all the aristocracy. Sober fact has it otherwise but much worse. The causes of the Revolution are of no great matter here but the effects of it are inescapable. The field was now reversed and those havens of transplanted English Catholicity where victims of conscience had sheltered for two centuries were themselves assaulted and their inhabitants expelled. The French Church itself witnessed scenes evocative of Tudor England. Two hundred priests and three bishops were massacred in a week. Eight hundred and fifty priests were imprisoned in old slave ships where conditions were so appalling as to merit the name "dry guillotine" from which only two hundred and seventy-four survived. Nuns met with similar brutality. The Recollects and Carmelites at Arras went to execution singing the Vespers of the dead, the Sacramentines of Bollene kissed the scaffold, the Ursulines of Valenciennes sang the *Te Deum* and forgave their killers as they lined-up for execution. Protestant England recoiled in horror and offered a hand of friendship and a place of refuge to thousands fleeing from such atrocities.

In the early days it was hoped that English institutions might escape the terror, but when Republican France went to war with England in 1793, any such hopes withered. All the houses of English religious mentioned earlier in this chapter managed by some means or other to get back to England. If not exactly welcomed home the recent changes in the law meant they could at least be tolerated. Two of these establishments are of importance to us because over the remaining years of our story, either directly or indirectly, they were going to educate the clergy who would serve Little Crosby. Most of the Benedictines of St. Laurence's, Dieulouard, dressed as laymen escaped in the nick of time. Their Prior, Richard Marsh of Hindley, having no pass, swam the River Moselle and rejoined his community via Germany. After nine years of wandering from place to place in England, they settled in Yorkshire, at Ampleforth, in 1802.

The English College at Douai was less fortunate at first. Ten professors and about thirty of the seminarists were imprisoned at Doullens for nearly two years and eventually returned to England dressed in rags. The College then divided, the southern students going to St. Edmund's College, Ware, Hertfordshire, those from the north making their way first to Crook Hall near Durham, then in 1808 occupying the purpose-built college of St. Cuthbert, Ushaw. (19)

The First Benedictine at Crosby

When the Benedictines accepted the care of Little Crosby in 1786 the rule was that their President-General could call upon any subject of any house to fill whatever vacancy there was. The system of parishes being allocated to specific monasteries only dates from 1891. The fact that nearly all the Benedictines who served Little Crosby were monks of Ampleforth is therefore really nothing more than coincidence. But the first of them all belonged to the Abbey of Lambspring in Hanover. He was Fr. Charles (Boniface in religion) Taylor, born at Goosnargh near Preston in 1752. Educated, and professed at Lambspring on 1 November, 1772, he served at Whitehaven until 1780, at Aberford near Leeds until 1786, then at Little Crosby until his death on 27 April, 1812. Subsequent to the Relief Act of 1791 he registered the West Lane chapel as a place of worship and himself as its authorised minister. In 1801 he began keeping the Baptismal Register and within twelve months recorded nine baptisms from Little Crosby, six from Great Crosby and three from Thornton. First of all was Mary Rymmer of Little Crosby followed by Robert Bond, Robert Westhead, Mary Formby and Jane Alty. He also recorded that bench rents brought in £7 a year, that he paid two guineas for a watch, that a maid's wages cost nineteen shillings a quarter and that £15 was sent to the bank. (20)

18th century Catholic piety was temperate. Controversy was thought to be best avoided, charity and good neighbourliness were encouraged. Great importance was placed upon the virtues of honesty, truthfulness, chastity and patience and nightly examination of conscience was considered essential. The prayers from *The Garden of the Soul*, a treasured possession of those who were able to read were highly acclaimed, one of which, as beautiful for its theological accuracy as for its spirit of calm resignation, brings us to a fitting epilogue.

"O my God, I accept of death as a homage and adoration which I owe to thy divine Majesty, as a punishment justly due to my sins; in union with the death of my dear Redeemer, and as the only means of coming to Thee, my beginning and last end."

CHAPTER 3

At Home and Abroad

NOTES

(1) W.R. Brownlow, *A Short History of the Catholic Church in England* (London 1897) pp 405-414; C.M. Carty and L. Rumble, "Intellectuals and Dogma" in *Eucharistic Quizzes* (Rockford, Illinois 1976) p2; R.W. Church, *The Oxford Movement* (London 1891); H. Foley, *Records of the English Province of the Society of Jesus* 8 vols. (London 1883) Vol 1, pp76-86; B. Palmer, *Reverend Rebels* (London 1993).

(2) B.W. Kelly, *Historical Notes on English Catholic Missions* (London 1907) p70, p208 and p376.

(3) C. Haigh, *Reformation and Resistance in Tudor Lancashire* (Cambridge 1975) p250; C. McCoog, *English and Welsh Jesuits* 1555 - 1650 Catholic Record Society vols 74 and 75 (1994 - 1995); G. Anstruther, *The Seminary Priests* 4 vols. (Great Wakering 1968 - 1977) Vol 1, Elizabethan.

(4) P. Guilday, *The English Catholic Refugees on the Continent* 1558-1795 (London 1914).

(5) J.C. Almond, *History of Ampleforth Abbey* (London 1903); B. Green, *The English Benedictine Congregation* (London 1979) p 32.

(6) F.O. Blundell, *Old Catholic Lancashire* 3 vols. (London 1925 - 1941) Vol 3, pp193 - 240).

(7) B. Basset, *The English Jesuits from Campion to Martindale* (London 1967); R.G. Dottie, "John Crosse of Liverpool and Recusancy in Early 17th Century Lancashire" in *Recusant History* vol.20, May 1990, p42.

(8) Foley; F. Tyrer, *The Great Diurnal of Nicholas Blundell* 3 vols. (Lancashire and Cheshire Record Society 1968) Vol 1.

(9) *Diurnal* Vol 1; Guilday p333.

(10) *Diurnal* Vol 1; M. Bence-Jones, *The Catholic Families* (London 1992) p29.

(11) *Diurnal* Vol 1; A.J. Mitchinson *The Return of Papists for The Diocese of Chester,* 1705 (Wigan 1986) pp 10-12.

(12) *Diurnal* Vol 1.

(13) A. Hewitson, *History of Preston* (Preston 1883); F. McLynn, *The Jacobites* (London 1985); F. Tyrer, *Recusancy of The Blundell Family and Inhabitants of Little Crosby,* Crosby Library C949.72 Cro, ms. in which the entire register of estates is transcribed.

(14) *Diurnal* Vol 2.

(15) *Diurnal* Vol 2; F. Tyrer, *The Blundell of Crosby Family - A Short Illustrated History* (Crosby 1960) pp 36-37.

(16) K. and D. Guest, *British Battles* (London 1996) pp 180-202; F. Tyrer, ms. Crosby Library C949.72 Cro, p426; P. Hughes, *The Catholic Question* (London 1929).

(17) Foley Vol 7 'Part the Second'; E.S. Worrall, *Return of Papists* 1767, *Diocese of Chester* (Catholic Record Society 1980) pp 43-45.

(18) Bassett; Hughes.

(19) D. Holmes, *The Triumph of The Holy See* (London 1978) pp 32-34; D. Milburn, *A History of Ushaw College* (Durham 1964); B. Ward, *History of St. Edmund's College* (London 1893).

(20) Crosby Library: Little Crosby Registers (photocopy).

CHAPTER 4

The Catholic Revival

"The effect which the events of those days produced upon thousands of Catholics in England was like the first fine days of spring after a long and dreary winter."

William J. Amherst
History of Catholic Emancipation, 1879.

In the year 1798 the trustees of the Little Crosby estate made some very wise investments by purchasing lands from the Molyneux of Sefton family and from the Earl of Derby. These transactions were carried out by trustees because the owner himself, William Joseph Blundell, was only twelve years old, his father, Nicholas Blundell having died in 1795. (1)

The 19th Century

As William grew up and as the new century developed, he took a great interest in the village and surrounding area. It is recorded that around 1800 Little Crosby as well as having agricultural workers, contained fishermen who gathered good harvests of shrimps, flukes and cockles. The land, very flat, was divided into meadows and pastures by ditches rather than hedges. The road to Great Crosby was lined by tall hedges on either side for a century more, and to travel to Liverpool meant either a lengthy walk across Seaforth sands to Great Howard Street, or taking a boat from Ford and arriving an hour later at Leeds Street, the terminus of the Leeds to Liverpool canal. (2)

William Blundell re-sited the village mill on the Moor Lane, built in its place the Liverpool Lodge of Crosby Hall and enclosed the entire property with the present long stone walls. In 1809 he married Catherine, daughter of Sir Thomas Massey-Stanley, of Hooton, Wirral. The Masseys came with William the Conqueror and settled at Dunham Massey in Cheshire. From the 13th century they had lived at Puddington, not far from Hooton. In the 17th century their chaplain, Fr. John Pleasington, was martyred at Chester, a victim of the Titus Oates conspiracy and is now a canonised saint. When their last survivor died in 1717 he bequeathed his estate to his godson, Thomas Stanley of Hooton, with the injunction to add the name of Massey to his own. Thus were two ancient Catholic families united. William and Catherine had eleven children, some born at Little Crosby, some at Brussels and some at Versailles near Paris. (3)

Pastoral Care

After the death of Fr. Taylor in 1812 the Little Crosby mission, as it was now identified, was officially vacant for nearly five years. But the Baptismal register was constantly maintained, entirely in the same hand-writing. Regrettably no signature was ever appended but there is reason to believe it to have been Fr. John Bede Rigby, OSB, then attached to St. Mary's Liverpool.

In 1817 Fr. James Calderbank, OSB came and signed for the first time on 22 June. He was born in Liverpool in 1770 and professed at Dieulouard in 1792. He escaped the French terror by fleeing to Trier where he was ordained priest in 1793. He then accompanied his homeless community on its several migrations - to Acton Burnell in Shropshire, to the Tranmere Hotel, Birkenhead, to Vernon Hall, Liverpool, but before they finally settled at Ampleforth he had been sent to Bath as resident priest, in 1800. After one year (1805) at Weston, Buckinghamshire, he was placed at St. Peter's, Seel Street, Liverpool. From 1809 to 1817 he was at Bath again from where he came to Little Crosby. In 1819 he moved to Woolton which was considered one of the best of the Benedictine's houses, long the residence of their President General. He died there on 9 April, 1821 and is buried in the vaults of St. Peter's Seel Street.

His successor at Little Crosby was Fr. Edward Benedict Glover OSB, born at Prescot on 4 March, 1787. He received the habit at Ampleforth in 1803 and was ordained on 6 February, 1811. He was assistant priest at St. Mary's, Liverpool before coming to Little Crosby. The fifteen years he spent here were to witness some exceptional events, locally and nationally. On 10 November, 1821, the Vicar Apostolic, Bishop Smith confirmed 133 persons in the West Lane Chapel. On 3 November, 1825, Bishop Penswick, coadjutor Vicar Apostolic, confirmed another 77. Their names were Alcock, Arnold, Bell, Bellion, Billington, Blanchard, Blundell, Carefoot, Cadice, Coppull, Davies, Fleetwood, Gilbertson, Halewood, Lovelady, Lupton, McNulty, Massam, Morley, Rainford, Swift, Westhead, Wharton and Wright.

In 1825 there were 18 baptisms of children from Great Crosby and one from Litherland. This, together with the optimistic climate of the times prompted the Vicar Apostolic to sanction a new mission for Great Crosby. So in 1826, SS Peter and Paul became independent, with its own church and resident priest. (4)

Catholic Emancipation

We have seen how repressive laws drove families like the Blundells, and many less influential ones, into recusancy. From 1559 to 1723 penalties had been devised and enforced with the intention of exterminating Catholicism. But by 1767 there were still 60,000 known Catholics and in 1825 there was half a million of them. Having granted forms of toleration in 1778 and in 1791, the Protestant ascendancy had for thirty years been divided as to whether to acknowledge or re-conquer this phenomenon that refused to go away.

The presence of many French refugees had done much to convince the average English person that Catholicism was not as abhorrent as many of them had been led to suppose. But one cynical observer had remarked "The Government which so willingly provided them with lodging, soap, crucifix, missal, beads and holy water, did so in the spirit that had they been Turks it would have given them coffee, opium, Korans and seraglios." (5)

About 1808 the Government began to make enquiries as to what degree of loy-alty might be expected in exchange for further relief. What was envisaged was some form of mild State control, especially over the appointment of bishops and teachers. The word veto was even mentioned. At this, John Milner, Vicar Apos-tolic of the Midland District, a man well known for his abrasive vocabulary, ex-celled himself. "Those subtle malignants - he said - will contrive to make every one of the episcopal qualities clash with their loyalty, and continue objecting until they get their immoral blockhead, their drunken infidel or their cringing tale-bear-ing sycophant consecrated." So nothing happened for another fifteen years and then when it did the impetus came from Ireland. By then while Protestant opposi-tion remained extreme Bishop Milner was a spent force.

There were at that time 220,000 Irish Catholics eligible to vote but as the law stood they could never elect a Catholic Member of Parliament. However there was nothing to prevent a Catholic from contesting a seat. In the person of Daniel O'Connell (1774 - 1847) a brilliant, honey-tongued lawyer, from Kerry came the very man. Repeatedly elected for Ennis, County Clare, he was disbarred because of his refusal to take the Oath of Supremacy. All Ireland was seething with political discontent. In 1828, the Duke of Wellington, who had led the British to victory at the Battle of Waterloo and was privately impressed with the eternal resilience of the Catholic Church, became Prime Minister. But he had told everyone he would never permit Catholic Emancipation. Face to face with a gruesome political deci-sion - revolution in Ireland or Catholic Emancipation - he picked, in his own words, "the lesser of two evils." This is, of course, a very simplified version of events. Several groups abroad observed with interest. In Italy, Germany, France and the United States there were numerous supporters and from these sources O'Connell received £28,000 towards his campaign. There was a great danger of matters getting out of hand when demands far more extreme than being permit-ted a voice in the affairs of State were raised.

In a month of almost daily sittings the Cabinet heard every conceivable shade of opinion from suggestions to deal directly with the Pope to demands for the resto-ration of the Penal Laws. Eventually, after two five hour meetings with King George IV, who believed himself to be in danger of violating the Coronation Oath, Wellington secured the Royal Assent to an Act that granted Catholics, with certain reservations, Emancipation. It became law on 13 April, 1829 and while none could have possibly foreseen it, nearly a century later a Blundell of Crosby was to be instrumental in securing the removal of most of those remaining reservations. (6)

The state of Catholicism in west Lancashire in 1829 is demonstrated in the following table.

PLACE	NUMBER OF CATHOLICS	REMARKS
Little Crosby	350	No Sects of any description
Altcar	122	
Great Crosby	471	1 Catholic Chapel
Formby	525	1 Catholic Chapel
Ince Blundell	449	1 Catholic Chapel
Litherland	78	3 Baptists
Lunt	10	
Lydiate	245	1 Catholic Chapel
Maghull	108	
Melling	75	
Netherton	24	1 Catholic Chapel
Ormskirk	200	50 Presbyterians 1 Chapel, 50 Methodists 1 Chapel and 100 Independents 1 Chapel
Orrell and Ford	200	Remainder are of the Established Church
Sephton	46	
Thornton	146	

In Liverpool there were 12,000 Catholics in 1821, 60,000 in 1831 and 80,000 in 1840. In Lancashire generally something like a hundred new Catholic churches were opened between 1830 and 1880. (7)

William Blundell, the Founder

William Blundell was described as "extremely capable, of determined nature, loved by friends, tenants and servants." He became a Justice of the Peace and Deputy Lieutenant of the County of Lancashire. He was the first Catholic to be High Sheriff of the County since the Reformation, but always refused to sit for a portrait. The only known existing sketch, complete with spectacles, top hat and umbrella, was made unknown to him, while he was watching the ships at Liverpool. A man of great personal loyalty as of deep faith, when Ampleforth was passing through a traumatic period in the 1820's he resolutely refused to remove his children to the rival and more fashionable Prior Park.

He made the first positive move towards the building of a church in 1839 by looking at some of the newly built ones. St. Anne's Anglican church at Rainhill impressed him considerably and he enquired as to its architect and its cost. He also admired old St. Marie's, Southport, St. Anne's, Edge Hill and St. Mary's, New Mills, Derbyshire. He travelled by steamer from Liverpool to view churches at Runcorn and by coach and railway to see others around Stockport. He did not care for St. Wilfrid's, Hulme, or St. Francis Xavier's, Liverpool and made no comment whatsoever after a visit to St. Bartholomew's, Rainhill. His favourite of all, an opinion confirmed by two or three different inspections was St. Oswald's, Old Swan (demolished 1956, its spire alone being retained) the work of A.W.N. Pugin, father of the Gothic Revival in England. Pugin was warmly recommended to Mr. Blundell by Dr. Youens, head priest of the old pro-cathedral of St. Nicholas, Liverpool. But after dealings with a Mr. Welch and a Mr. Sharpe, who actually produced plans in December 1842, on 26 April, 1844 Matthew Ellison Hadfield was engaged as architect. (8)

The Founder

Hadfield

Born at Glossop in 1812, his father was Joseph Hadfield. His mother, Mary Ellison, was sister of the Duke of Norfolk's Sheffield agent. Her mother was Elizabeth Worthy of Ince Blundell. Educated at Mr. Robinson's School, Woolton, Liverpool and trained as an architect in Doncaster and London, he entered into a partnership with John Gray Weightman and their numerous commissions carried their reputation throughout Lancashire and Yorkshire, into Lincolnshire and across to Ireland. St. John's Cathedral, Salford, St. Marie's Cathedral, Sheffield, the Great Northern Hotel, Leeds and the Gorton Depot on the Lancashire and Yorkshire Railway being among them. For a time George Goldie, who was later to be architect of Our Lady's, Formby, was also with their firm.

Matthew Hadfield became an Associate of the Royal Institute of British Architects in May, 1847 and was a member of its governing council. Always an ardent Catholic, his two daughters became nuns, one a Sister of Charity in London, the other a Sister of the Sacred Heart in Brighton. He died in 1885. (9)

The Site

Mr. Blundell desired and Mr. Hadfield concurred that the place known locally as The Hill should be the site of the proposed church. This was a slightly elevated position above the village, close to where the Back Lane became the road to Altcar.

Little Crosby Quarry had yielded plentiful red sandstone since the 17th century. Much used in extensions to the Hall and in building local cottages, it was tested for suitability as material for the new church by a pillar being made from it. This was erected at Delph Farm and left to see if it would retain its colour and withstand the seasons. It did so, and on 18 March, 1845, Mr. Hollins, the building contractor and three workmen began preparing the ground.

Foundation Stone Laid

On the feast of the Annunciation, 25 March, 1845 the Foundation Stone of the new church was blessed and laid, amidst great rejoicing. Bishop George Brown, Vicar Apostolic of the Lancashire District, performed the Ceremony in the presence of Bishop Sharples, his coadjutor and the entire Little Crosby community. Also present were Frs. Shann (Little Crosby), Brown (Great Crosby), Smith (Formby), Greenough (Ince Blundell), Abram (Netherton) and Clough S.J. (Liverpool). The neighbouring family of Weld-Blundell was well represented but regrettably the Founder himself could not take part because he was serving as Foreman of the Jury at Preston Assizes. But he was represented by his eldest son, Nicholas, who received from the tenants a silver trowel to commemorate the occasion. (10)

We do not know what the Vicar Apostolic actually said at the event. He might have referred to it as being symptomatic of the enormous progress that Catholicity was enjoying generally. St. Edward's College Liverpool had opened in 1843 and the Sisters of Notre Dame had just arrived to open a school and an orphanage. In 1845 the bishop himself solemnly consecrated new and worthy churches at Kirkham near Preston and at Blackbrook, St. Helens and in Liverpool itself. Several more were in the course of erection. No one could have been aware that far away in Oxford, an influential Anglican clergyman, Rector of the University Church and much respected for his learning and holiness of life, was battling with his conscience as to whether or not he too should join the Catholic Church. On 9 October, 1845 he did so. His name was John Henry Newman and in 1879 he became a Cardinal. The events that led Newman and many others to such a decision were to have so profound an effect upon English Catholicism as to give it an identity that would endure for another hundred years. St. Mary's, Little Crosby would so splendidly typify this, therefore such events cannot be ignored at this point.

The Oxford Movement

While the English Catholics were getting used to their newly acquired liberties and William Blundell was contemplating the new church for Little Crosby, the political scene internationally was such that many believed the old systems of Monarchy and aristocratic rule were to be banished forever, by revolutionary methods if necessary. The year 1848 has been called "the year of revolution" because almost every nation in Europe rebelled over some discontentment or other. England escaped only narrowly. Thousands of Chartists assembled in London, not rejecting the possibility of armed insurrection. The astute had long seen all this coming and their greatest dread had been that the horrendous events of the French Revolution might be repeated here. So they began to examine any avenue or institution that might help stave off such an undesirable thing. In Oxford a group of serious minded scholars, with these anxieties in mind, began to look at the nature of the Church. They knew that in medieval times the Church had been a power in the land, able to command respect and enforce discipline. But what they discovered was that the part of it that Henry VIII and his successors had separated from the Universal Church had degenerated into a moribund arm of the Civil Service that few took seriously. And of those who did, many were regarded as unintelligent and eccentric even by their own bishops.

The Oxford group developed the idea of re-Catholicising the Church of England from within. This resulted in the building of vast Gothic churches, the use of Roman practices including confession and the wearing of vestments and burning incense. Saints days were revived and such terminology as the word mass and addressing the clergy as father was encouraged. There was much bitter reaction as this High Church element almost created a church within a church. Some like Newman believed that the Church of England could never be Catholicised and left it. Some remained, only to be penalised for their efforts while others were pushing orthodoxy to its very limits, and in one or two cases well beyond, but were untouchable in law. A clergyman named Gorham taught that there was no difference between a baptised person and an unbaptised one. He was censured by his bishop for doing so but the bishop was overruled by the Privy Council. Many more left at this point, the future Cardinal Manning among them. This was in 1850, at the time that Pope Pius IX was restoring the Catholic hierarchy to England and Wales. Reaction to this "Papal aggression" led, in some places, to rioting and looting. Manning was dismayed that people who would riot in the streets over what was nothing more than ecclesiastical nomenclature, saw no relevance at all in the doctrine concerning the sacrament of baptism. (11)

Faith of Our Fathers

Frederick William Faber was another of these famous converts. He became a priest in the London Oratory and wrote such spiritual classics as *All for Jesus, Bethlehem, The Blessed Sacrament, The Foot of The Cross* and *The Precious Blood*. These are weighty volumes of four hundred pages apiece. He also wrote many famous hymns including *Jesus My Lord My God My All, O Purest of Creatures* and what was virtually to become the Catholic national anthem, *Faith of Our Fathers*.

The new converts, of whom there were many, were not greatly impressed by the remnant of Catholicism that three centuries of persecution had reduced it to in England. English Catholicism at that time was , of necessity and by habit, discreet in presentation and sober in piety. But the converts loved Rome where prolonged public devotions to the Blessed Sacrament, masses of candles burning around costly shrines, processions, novenas and exotic practices such as the Stations of the Cross abounded. They also had a most intense admiration for the person of the Pope. Such was their influence that they were able to introduce, some might say impose, these innovations into England just at the time that St. Mary's, Little Crosby was new. Within twenty years such things had become normal practice here. Within a lifetime they had become traditional. (12)

It might be added that when on 29 September, 1850 Pope Pius IX restored the hierarchy to England and Wales, the western part of Lancashire (76 miles from the Mersey to Lake Windermere, 28 miles Formby Point to Astley) comprised the new diocese of Liverpool, with the Vicar Apostolic, George Brown as first bishop. By that decree the old days of suppressed missionary activity came to an end and a new era of the Church regulated from Rome commenced.

St. Mary's is Built

It cannot be claimed that the building of St. Mary's proceeded without problems. By May 1845 Mr. Hollin's two workmen, their work strongly but roughly done, were dismissed and ten more taken on in their place. By September work had progressed as far as the chancel arch which on examination was found to be an inch and a half out of perpendicular. But its rebuilding provided an opportunity for lengthening the sanctuary by eighteen inches. Mr. Blundell had asked the architect if he might incorporate something of the spire of Aughton Church into his design. When approaching from Back Lane and passing the presbytery, it looks as if, consciously or otherwise, he was influenced by the spire of Sefton Church too.

With the exception of the spire, building was completed by December 1845. By the end of February 1846 the spire was completed and the weathercock positioned. Attention then moved to the question of heating the building. Plasterers

and glaziers arrived and Stafford tiles were purchased to cover the sanctuary floor. The bell was installed on 3 July, 1846. It cost £55, £18 of which was raised by public collections and £25 donated by a Miss Lacon or Leecon. Estate workers prepared the surrounding cemetery and by a tragic coincidence, Thomas Blundell, the twenty year old son of the Founder was the first to be buried there on 1 March, 1847. (13)

Practicalities

On 19 August, 1847, Fr. Henry A Brewer OSB, came from Liverpool to Crosby Hall to discuss with Mr. Blundell the details concerning the solemn consecration of a church. This, it must be understood, differs considerably from the ordinary blessing that is given to any newly built church. Solemn consecration may only be performed if the church stands on freehold land and is unencumbered by debt. Some churches have to wait for years to achieve this status and in 1847 there was barely a dozen of them in all England.

The ceremony itself lasted about four hours. It consisted of processions both inside and outside the church, the Greek and Latin alphabets had to be traced, in incense, in the form of a St. Andrews Cross across its floor, by the bishop using the tip of his crozier. The interior walls were anointed and fourteen crosses and candle sconces erected to mark the places. Relics authenticated by Rome had to be sealed inside the altar and all was accompanied by the chanting of psalms and readings from scripture - in Latin of course.

On 21 August, 1847 Mr. Blundell wrote to the Vicar Apostolic asking what was an appropriate salary for the priest to be attached to the new church and furthermore who had the right of selecting the priest for such appointment. The reply stated that Canon Law specified the amount and that he - Mr. Blundell - had the right to appoint. Later, in 1861 this latter point was denied by Bishop Goss who claimed that all lay patronage had been abolished at the restoration of the hierarchy. Had the then patron, Colonel Nicholas Blundell, contested this he may well have won the case because several such examples could have been given well after 1850. But everything appears to have worked out amicably and good relations have always existed between presbytery and Hall.

On 30 August, 1847 Mr. Blundell drove to Ormskirk to ask Fr. George Alban Caldwell OSB, to preach at the opening of St. Mary's which had been fixed for Wednesday, 8 September, 1847. A decade later this same Fr. Caldwell was to serve Little Crosby for three years, 1856 - 1859. (14)

Solemn Consecration of St. Mary's

On Tuesday, 7 September 1847, the church was solemnly consecrated to Almighty God under the title of the Blessed Virgin Mary, by Bishop Brown, Vicar Apostolic of the Lancashire District. Bishop Sharples, his coadjutor, and all the neighbour-ing clergy and many of the villagers were present at the ceremony which com-menced at eight-thirty and lasted until noon. Other distinguished guests included the Earl of Arundel, Lady Smythe and her daughters from Acton Burnell in Shrop-shire, Charles and Monica Tempest from Skipton and members of the Salvin and Trafford families. The first Mass in the newly consecrated church was celebrated by its resident priest, Fr. Christopher A. Shann, OSB.

The following day - Our Lady's Birthday - saw the formal opening to the public and several more guests arrived. The Stanleys from Hooton, the Mostyns from Talacre and Sir Arnold Knight and his two sons, one of whom was destined to become second Bishop of Shrewsbury. The first High Mass was celebrated by Bishop Brown with Rev. Dr. Thomas Youens (St. Nicholas', Liverpool) as deacon and Abbot Alban Molineau OSB (St. Alban's, Warrington) as sub-deacon. Fr. Robert Chapman (St. Werburgh, Birkenhead) was assistant priest and Fr. Peter Greenough (Ince Blundell) was Master of Ceremonies. Dr. Youens preached and a choir of twenty-three priests from south Lancashire, Cheltenham, Preston and the Wirral sang. Fr. Caldwell, OSB preached at Solemn Vespers in the evening.

In all about £2,500 was spent on the building and furnishing of St. Mary's. Trans-lated into present day values that is at least £160,000. Mr. William Blundell's gen-erosity was augmented by that of the Massey - Stanley family. In the immediate future more was to be expended upon its upkeep and decoration, while its com-manding position, open to the strong winds from the North and the Irish sea, was to make constant maintenance an additional expense. The spire also became a favourite nesting place for jackdaws. (15)

Priests and People (1)

Fr. Glover last signed the baptismal register at West Lane, Little Crosby on 7 March, 1834 and died the following 14 May. He had published two books *An Explanation of the Mass* and *An Explanation of the Sacraments*. He also wrote several articles for the old *Catholic Magazine*.

From 21 March, 1834 to 27 September, 1835, Little Crosby was served by Fr. William Bernard Allen Collier OSB. Born at Leyburn, Yorkshire in 1803, a monk of Douai he was clearly destined for high office. He became Prior of Douai at the age of 23 and after eighteen months at West Lane he became Procurator of the English Benedictine Congregation and lived in Rome. In 1840 he was made Vicar Apostolic of Mauritius, an Anglo-French colony in the Indian ocean where pesti-lence and hurricanes were part of everyday life. But he lived to the age of 87.

He was succeeded at Little Crosby by Fr. William Jerome Hampson OSB, a na-tive of Ashton-under-Lyne and a monk of Ampleforth who remained until 2 Sep-tember, 1838 when he moved to Knaresborough.

Fr. James Hilary Dowding, OSB came next and had the distinction of serving here at two separate periods. Firstly at West Lane from 1838 to 1843 and later at St. Mary's from 1850 to 1856. He also had the distinction of having been married. Born at Bath in 1793 he joined the Ampleforth community after the death of his wife in 1832. Having completed the noviciate many years earlier, he was advanced to ordination in 1834 and made sub-prior of Ampleforth. From there he came to Little Crosby and then held subsequent appointments in Cheltenham, Ormskirk and Grassendale where he died in 1864.

Fr. Christopher Austin Shann, OSB born at Knaresborough in 1801 also served Little Crosby twice, from 1843 to 1850 and again from 1858 to 1860. Hence he was the first resident priest at St. Mary's. After Fr. Dowding's second term there came Fr. George Alban Caldwell, OSB, a native of Warrington, born in 1806, ordained at Ampleforth in 1830. He served St. Peter's, Liverpool on two separate occasions and St. Bede's, Clayton Green for five years, 1834 to 1839. From 1844 to 1856 he was rector of St. Anne's, Ormskirk and responsible for the erection of the present fine church there in 1850. After two years at Little Crosby he moved to the tiny mission of Lee House, Longridge and finally, in 1868, went to St. Benet's, Netherton where he died in 1870.

The last marriage in the old West Lane chapel was that of Thomas Parker and Mary Billington. The first in St. Mary's was that of Charles Jones and Margaret Lathom. The first baptism in St. Mary's was that of Henry Halewood, son of Thomas and Isabella formerly Wharton. After the interment of young Thomas Blundell, already described, the first parishioner to be buried at St. Mary's was Joseph Spencer on 27 October, 1847.

An examination of the mid - 19th century census returns reveals that only about half the population of Little Crosby was actually born there. It is true that there were the large indigenous farming families of Bond, Gilbertson, Heptonstall, Rainford and Wright. But others came from Dover, Hereford, Liverpool, Melton Mowbray, Poulton-le-Fylde, Preston, Warwickshire, Worcester and Wales. There were a few Irish farm workers, the local blacksmith came from Skelmersdale, the clogger from Prescot and the keeper of the lighthouse at Hightown was born on the island of Orkney. (16)

The Decoration of St. Mary's

William Blundell the Founder had eleven children. Nicholas, his eldest son and eventual successor was the animator of most of the interior decoration of the church. His sisters Fanny and Annie (who later became a nun) assisted him. Another son, John Blundell married Catherine Middleton of Myddleton Lodge, Ilkley and farmed at Crook Hall, near Leyland. Their son became Fr. Frederick Odo Blundell, OSB, author of the three volumes *Old Catholic Lancashire* published

The Sanctuary, 1997

between 1925 and 1941. Yet another son of the founder, William (born 18 February 1816), became a captain in the army and was killed at Rangoon in 1852. The above mentioned John made a very attractive etching of St. Mary's in 1849.

Nicholas Blundell, in his own workshop and with his own hands, carved a Paschal candlestick from Caen stone, made the panelling for the confessional, painted the background for the Christmas crib and carved pedestals and canopies for the statues. The statues of Our Lady and St. John the Evangelist were by Karl Hoffmann (1816 - 1872) of Cologne who also made the bas-relief of the *Descent from the Cross*.

Nicholas also made an etching of St. Mary's from the exterior in 1849 and was a musician sufficiently accomplished to reduce the Masses of Mozart and Haydn for performance by the village choir. However, his most famous contribution was undoubtedly his design and execution of the Litany of Loreto, painted in blue, red and gold. This runs the length of the ceiling from chancel arch to choir loft and contains the entire litany as then known, from Sancta Maria (Holy Mary) to Regina Sanctorum Omnium (Queen of all Saints). It was cut to a stencil, painted on canvas and finally attached to the plaster. But the years took their toll and deterioration grew obvious. In 1977 the lettering was renewed by the school head-mistress, Mrs. Claire Barnes, but regrettably the scene above the chancel arch - Christ in Glory - also believed to be the work of Nicholas Blundell, could not be rescued from decay. (17)

Consolidation

A few weeks after the opening of St. Mary's, work commenced on the demolition of the old chapel at West Lane. But it was only partially accomplished and about ten years later that historic property was converted into a convent and school.

A new house for the priest had always been part of Mr. Hadfield's original scheme. This house was first occupied in 1850 when the Arms of Blundell of Crosby were placed above its threshold but two more years elapsed before its paths were levelled and paved and its front steps were put there.

As in old Catholic times the fields opposite this house were granted to the priest as glebelands and as late as 1920 his crop of withens was marketed around Lydiate and Maghull and made into hampers. A shippon for his animals was also built.

It is clear from Nicholas Blundell's diary that liturgical practice in those early years was correct and expertly performed. He himself sometimes acted as thurifer. There was Midnight Mass at Christmas, the Holy Week ceremonies were complete with altar of repose and procession, singing Popule Meus during the veneration of the cross and an Easter Sepulchre. Solemn High Mass, which required the participation of three priests, was made possible on the greater feasts by assistance of visitors from Great Crosby or Liverpool. The choir built up a reasonable repertoire of music, some of which was damaged by flooding from the spire during a great storm on 27 October, 1880. The organ, which is still in use, was purchased from Fr. Ralph Wilfrid Cooper, OSB, of St. Anne's, Edge Hill, in 1847.

Nicholas and his mother and his sister Catherine were present at the stone-laying ceremony on 31 March, 1854 of the new church of Our Lady, Lydiate, built through the generosity of Thomas Weld - Blundell. (18)

Death of the Founder

On 11 July, 1854, the founder of St. Mary's, Little Crosby, William Joseph Blundell, died at Taunton, Somerset at the age of 68. The village and the entire neighbourhood mourned its sudden loss. The church was immediately draped in black, by Woolwrights of Liverpool, and on 18 July, 15 priests attended in cassock and surplice while three others, principally Fr. Dowding, OSB, the rector, sang Solemn Requiem Mass. The choir's rendition of the *De Profundis* attracted special mention. The body was carried to its vault by representatives of servants and tenants and in November 1855 the tomb was erected on the left-hand side of the sanctuary. Its figure, in Caen stone, is described as an admirable likeness. The three accompanying shields carry the arms of (1) Blundell of Crosby (2) Stanley of Hooton (3) Blundell of Crosby impaling arms of Stanley. (19)

The New Squire

We already know about the faith and artistic talents of Nicholas Blundell who was now to hold the Manor of Little Crosby for forty years. Born there on 22 April,

Col. Nicholas Blundell

1811 and baptised on the day of his birth, he was educated at Ampleforth. In 1847 he married Agnes Mary, daughter of Sir Edward Smythe, Bart. of Acton Burnell. They had nine children. Like his father, he became a Justice of the Peace and having attained the rank of Lieutenant-Colonel in the Duke of Lancaster's Own Rifle Militia, he was popularly referred to as "the Colonel." While devoted to Little Crosby and its traditions, he loved travelling and painted many scenes in Switzerland and Italy in addition to those nearer home.

Sisters of Charity

Squire Nicholas was inspired to bring a small community of nuns to teach in the village school and, if necessary, care for the sick. After some correspondence an offer was accepted by the Sisters of Charity at Sheffield to send three of their members to occupy part of the old West Lane House where an extension dating from 1782 was made into a small convent and school.

At two o'clock in the afternoon on 3 June, 1859 Sisters Tibault, Mary and Vincent arrived. After tea they were taken for a walk round the village and expressed themselves pleased with their new surroundings. (20)

The history of the order is of some interest. About 1633, the great apostle of charity, Vincent de Paul, attracted a group of women to assist in looking after the sick-poor and instructing the ignorant. He never foresaw that by the time of the great revolution, a hundred and sixty years ahead, they would have 6000 nuns in 425 houses. Indeed whenever such things were spoken of, he advised "Let your cell be the sick-room, your chapel the parish church, your enclosure the streets of the city, your grill the fear of God and your veil holy modesty." Practical necessity eventually compelled them to adopt a written constitution and their very distinctive dress of dark blue habit and white-starched, shoulder-width cornette (enormous sized hat) may still be visualised by many people.

During the French terror the good works of these nuns saved them from physical attack but they were expelled from all their schools and hospitals. However, persecution at home was the means of their dispersal throughout Europe and America (where their efforts were outstandingly successful), to Drogheda in 1855, to Sheffield in 1857 and to Little Crosby in 1859. Therefore their convent here was only their second foundation in England. (21) The ever generous Nicholas allocated them £1 per week for expenses and a constant supply of fruit, vegetables and coal. The superior was always referred to as *"Ma Soeur"* and later generations of parishioners well remembered Ma Soeur O'Grady and Sister Clare Quigley, who taught the boys and Sister Teresa Parker who taught the girls. The squire's sister, Annie, joined the order and became Sister Mary. As Ma Soeur Blundell she was superior at Dunmanaway, County Cork for many years. Other local girls also joined, notably Mary and Eleanor Rainford. Eleanor was still alive in 1958 having been a nun for seventy years. (22)

Death of Fr. Shann

On 25 April, 1860, the maid found Fr. Shann collapsed in his study as he sat reading the Divine Office. She rushed to Great Crosby and returned with Canon Fisher, who was just in time to anoint him at the very instant of his death. Large numbers assembled for the funeral at St. Mary's on 30 April. Four of his nephews from Yorkshire carried the coffin to burial in the churchyard after Fr. Greenough of Ince Blundell had offered Requiem Mass. Then after dinner at the Hall, the Benedictine Provincial, Fr. Athanasius Allanson, politely informed those present that he could no longer undertake the responsibility of supplying them with a priest. We shall never know what prompted such a decision. Relations between Nicholas Blundell and the Benedictines had always been cordial. It cannot be said they were short of vocations as it was, for them, a time of unprecedented missionary activity. New parishes were staffed by the monks throughout the north of England, south Wales and west Cumberland which was to be almost a Benedictine preserve. They were also making a massive contribution to building up the Church in Australia, indeed the second Archbishop of Sydney, Roger Bede Vaughan, OSB, died at Ince Blundell Hall in 1884 while visiting his relations there.

Perhaps Little Crosby was thought to be a shade too comfortable for men invigorated by the story of St. Augustine's conversion of England and convinced that what had been done once could be done again. Perhaps they were not particularly happy in dealing with a lay patron, for a similar withdrawal was to occur at Wrightington where the Dicconsons had achieved something akin to, though not identical with that of the Blundells. (23) Whatever the cause the effect was that for almost a year no priest could be found to serve this debt-free church in a near idyllic environment. Passionists from Sutton came on supply as did Franciscans from Pantasaph but on one particular Sunday, 10 June, 1860, the entire Little Crosby congregation was obliged to walk to Ince Blundell for Mass. In October some Belgian Franciscans expressed an interest but were not acceptable. The

Mother House of the Little Crosby nuns was at Sheffield where the priests were Vincentians. They offered a priest who was acceptable to Nicholas Blundell but not to Bishop Goss of Liverpool. The bishop, seemingly fearless of an important and generous patron, wrote that he had no intention of allowing a single member of an order not otherwise represented in the diocese to be appointed. He went on to say that whatever had been the arrangements in the old days of recusancy, times had changed and now he had the right to veto any such appointment.

Little Crosby was not the only place to experience this prelate's intransigence. After visiting Alston Lane, near Preston he said his reception had been scarcely civil and that he was looked upon as an intruder. At Blackbrook, St. Helens he said he would return with a folio volume of theology to convince them he was not being awkward or scrupulous. On 2 March, 1861 he sent Little Crosby a priest who was to make his reputation elsewhere, but he was learned and experienced. Many years later, after he was dead, his biography would be written, his statue would be erected in the centre of Liverpool and many people would revere him as a saint. His name was James Nugent. (24)

Priests and People (2)

One of Fr. Nugent's first tasks was the blessing and inauguration of the newly acquired Stations of the Cross - from Cotelle of Paris - on 25 March, 1861. He also enjoyed working in the garden and made the flower-holders from hewn-out tree trunks that once flanked the presbytery entrance. Fr. Nugent, born in Liverpool in 1822, was educated at Ushaw and Rome. Officially he was rector of the Catholic Institute, a school for boys in Hope Street, Liverpool. But having busied himself in countless worthy causes, not least visiting and in-structing the poor people in Brownlow Hill Work-house, he had been advised to rest. For this reason he was at Little Crosby from 1861 to 1863 when he went as the first full-time Catholic Chaplain to Walton Gaol. His name survives in the title of the Liverpool Archdiocesan Social Services of which he is rightly regarded as founder.

Fr. Henry Grey Bennett (Canon Bennett from 1878) came next. Born at Thomastown House, County Offaly in 1829, he had two brothers who were priests, Thomas of St. Oswald's, Old Swan and Albert of St. Thomas's, Waterloo. Educated at Ushaw and ordained in 1857, he was curate at Old Swan when appointed to Little Crosby. An accomplished pianist, he often entertained the peo-ple at the Hall or those from the village. He also

Fr. Nugent

composed the hymns that are still sung, every September, at the Harvest Festival. Under his own name Canon Bennett is characterised in the novel *In a North Country Village* by M.E. Francis. Little Crosby is also easily recognised but called Thornleigh. (25)

Canon Bennett

M.E. Francis was the pen-name of Mrs. Mary Blundell, wife of Francis Nicholas Blundell, the second son of Squire Nicholas, the Colonel. She was born Mary Sweetman at Lamberton Park, County Leix. Married in 1879 but widowed in 1884, possessing a talent for writing her first publications were pious short stories in Church magazines. In 1889 her novel *Molly's Fortune* was serialised in the *Irish Monthly*. This was followed by *In a North Country Village, The Story of Dan, A Daughter of the Soil, Maime O'the Corner, Frieze and Fustian, Miss Erin, The Duenna of a Genius* and *Yeoman Fleetwood*. These were works of approximately four hundred pages, published by Longmans Green and Company of Paternoster Row, London. Doubtless nowadays they would be dismissed as mere chronicles of Victorian rectitude where the virtues of the lowly inevitably triumph over the wrongs of the worldly-wise. But in their day they enjoyed tremendous popularity and can still fetch a fair price when they appear on a dealer's list. (26)

Early in 1887 Canon Bennett attended the ceremonial laying of the foundation stone at St. Joseph's, Blundellsands. Although unwell he called upon a sick parishioner, then took to his bed, developed pneumonia and died on 11 May. Although only 57 years of age his bearing and authority caused him to appear almost patriarchal in character. He was buried in St. Mary's churchyard in a spot that he himself had selected.

The parishioners at that time were named Billington, Blundell, Bristow, Brooks, Cowell, Forshaw, Gannon, Harrison, Jones, Kiernan, Lathom, Leatherbarrow, Lovelady, Makin, Massam, Morley, Newman, Orme, Rainford, Rimmer, Russell, Sykes, Waring and Warton. Benjamin Bristow had succeeded John Crook as coachman at Crosby Hall. John Crook's son returned many years later, as parish priest. The son of Charles Russell, a tailor, and his wife the former Alice Litherland also became a priest. Fr. William Russell was born at Little Crosby in 1884, ordained in 1909 but died (at St. Oswald's, Old Swan) at the early age of forty. From this Russell family is descended the Right Reverend Vincent Nichols, the present auxiliary bishop in Westminster.

A good account of contemporary domesticity exists. "The women took in washing. Food came from a family pig and a well-stocked garden. None worked on Sunday or Holydays of Obligation. Bank Holidays were ignored in favour of Church holidays. Canon Bennett had a white Pomeranian dog named Bruce who accompanied him everywhere, even into the sanctuary where a cushion was reserved for him." In reply to criticism the Canon would say, "I only wish many Christians were as innocent as poor Bruce!" The carters rose at 3 am to feed their horses and take their produce to market. However bitter the weather they had to travel at walking pace. At market or docks they would be surrounded by houses selling crude spirit that warmed the consumer, at very low prices. Sister Clare who was strictly teetotal would administer the pledge before the altar rails and say, "If you can do without it until you are 21 you can do without it altogether." (27)

From 1887 to 1892 St. Mary's was in the care of Fr. Michael J. McCarthy. Born at Youghal, County Cork on 20 November, 1854 and ordained at St. Patrick's College, Carlow in 1879, he was a curate at St. Mary's, Blackbrook and St. John's, Kirkham before coming here. We know very little else about him. In 1893 he was a curate again - at All Saints, Anfield - and later at St. James', Bootle. He then returned to Ireland. Fr. McCarthy was succeeded at St. Mary's by Fr. William Smith (later Canon) who survived well into the twentieth century.

Other Events

The feast of Corpus Christi was celebrated with an outdoor procession of the Blessed Sacrament. People wore their Sunday best, visiting clergy wore dalmatics and the banner of the Ince Blundell and Little Crosby Sick and Benevolent Society was carried.

During the American Civil War when the cotton manufacturing towns were at starvation point because no raw material was reaching them, the Colonel made door to door relief collections in the village.

On 16 June, 1871 the Pontifical Silver Jubilee of Pope Pius IX was celebrated in the grand tradition. At noon a royal salute of twenty-one guns was fired. In the afternoon games were played, tea was served and a band of musicians enlivened all. Rockets and other fireworks brought from Liverpool were spent and real cannons were fired. After dark VIVA PIO IX in illuminated letters was placed above the Liverpool Lodge. There had been some rain that day but not sufficient to dampen enthusiasm. Pope Pius IX was to live for seven more years and having reigned for thirty-two years experienced the longest pontificate in history. Despite much personal misfortune he had the highest regard for English Catholicism and often likened its resurgence from Penal Laws to the rising of Our Blessed Lord from the sepulchre - driven underground for a time but now returned, more glorious than before.

The death of Francis Nicholas Blundell on 27 April, 1884 at the age of 31 moved the Colonel, his father, to consider the building of a memorial chapel. At the time, Mr. A.E. Purdie, an architect of Brook Green, Hammersmith, was in the district making preparations for the new church of St. Joseph, Blundellsands. So the idea was discussed. Plans were drawn up, stone from the local quarry was used, and while such an opportunity was available, a new sacristy was also built. Work began on 20 November, 1885. The chapel roof was ready to be slated on 22 December. Completion was on 4 February, 1886 and the following July the statue of Our Lady of Lourdes was placed there. On 28 August, formal dedication as a memorial chapel took place. Fifty years later it would be redesigned as the English Martyr's Chapel.

Another interesting statue in the church is that of St. Roch, a fourteenth century Frenchman, rescued from starvation by a mysterious dog that daily carried bread to him in its mouth. He prayed that all who invoked his name against the plague would be cured and thus gained a reputation as the Patron Saint of infectious diseases. The statue was donated by Mary Blundell the novelist, after an epidemic of influenza had ravaged the district in the winter of 1889 - 1890. She had prayed daily to the saint and persuaded others to do so too.

On 10 January, 1890, Agnes Blundell, the Colonel's wife died while he himself was too ill to attend the funeral. Bishop O'Reilly of Liverpool (whose mother was Mary Blundell of Ince Blundell) offered Requiem Mass while, as was then the fashion, all the arches and the pulpit and altar rails were draped in black material.

The Colonel died at Teignmouth, near Torquay on 12 July, 1894 and was buried at Little Crosby on the 17th. The See of Liverpool was vacant because Bishop O'Reilly had died the previous April. So the Solemn Requiem Mass was sung by the Vicar Capitular, Mgr. James Carr, of Our Lady's, Formby. The church was overcrowded and Faith of Our Fathers was sung as the final procession to the grave was in progress.

Bishop O'Reilly had been ordained priest in 1847, the year that St. Mary's was opened. He had been Bishop of Liverpool since 1873. As previously stated his mother's family belonged to Ince Blundell and he never repressed his affection for the district. On one occasion, speaking about the hosts used in Holy Communion, he said he wished they could all be manufactured from wheat grown in the fields around Little Crosby that had been Catholic from time immemorial.

With these deaths of Bishop O'Reilly and Colonel Nicholas Blundell it was truly the end of an era. (28)

Victorian Catholicism

The Catholic Family Annual and Almanac for the Dioceses of Liverpool and Shrews-bury for the year 1900 was a handsome volume of 230 pages, costing sixpence (2.5p). It states that Little Crosby mission contained 600 Catholics served by Fr. William Smith. There were two Sunday Masses, at 8 and 10.30 am and Rosary and Benediction was at 3 in the afternoon. On Holydays of Obligation Mass was at 7.30 and 9.30 am and Benediction at 7.30 in the evening. There was Rosary and Benediction on Friday evenings at 7.30 and confessions were heard on Saturdays and the vigils of holydays from 4 to 5 pm and from 6 to 9 pm. The school, with 189 children, was staffed by the Sisters of Charity. Although completely redecorated in 1899 it received no annual grant from the Government. Furthermore we learn that the cemetery had been extended in 1896 and a new stained glass window placed on the south side of the sanctuary. Fr. Smith, it appears, thought if entertainment could not be provided locally, people would go to towns, and possibly into temptation, to find it, so a men's club and billiards room had been opened. Frank Tyrer says its front was built to resemble a house so that if needs be it could be converted into one; also that people who travelled from Hightown or other distances, left their ponies there while they attended Mass.

If Victorian Catholicism appeared to be somewhat florid externally, it was undoubtedly severe. The perfection of God and the sinfulness of Man were constantly brought into focus with prayer and penance as the necessary link. The Church imposed rigorous rules even to the degree that all who served on the altar or sang in the choir must be of unblemished reputation. Mass could not be celebrated later than midday. To receive Holy Communion it was necessary to be fasting from midnight. Fasting in another sense meant a day when only one full meal was allowed. With abstinence from meat and all its extracts, it was inseparable from Catholicism. All the weekdays of Lent were days of abstinence while Wednesdays and Fridays were days of fasting and abstinence - as was Christmas Eve. Every Friday of the year was a day of abstinence as were the vigils of certain great feasts. Marriages could not take place in Lent or from the beginning of Advent until after the Epiphany. To marry a non-Catholic meant the side altar or sacristy for the ceremony and to marry outside the Church was condemned as gravely sinful until 1908 and invalid afterwards. To participate in any form of non-Catholic worship carried a censure and to send a child to a non-Catholic school required a special dispensation which in the Liverpool diocese was rarely, if ever, given.

But the lives of many ordinary Catholics were an edification and an inspiration. Devotion to the Blessed Sacrament not only took the form of weekly Benediction but prolonged periods of prayer such as the Forty Hours exposition and seasonal processions. Frequent reception of Holy Communion only came later, indeed such was contemporary awe for the Real Presence that monthly Communion was thought adequate and silence as well as fasting was encouraged before it. To pray for the faithful departed was a necessary act of charity and indulgences to be gained on their behalf were plentiful. Likewise to remember one's own end and pray for a happy death merited a special litany in the prayer books and a special confraternity - *Bona Mors* - in the large towns.

The 19th century was pre-eminently the age of Mary who, honoured as the daughter of the Father, the mother of the Son and the spouse of the Holy Spirit was acknowledged as humanity's direct involvement in the life of the Holy Trinity itself, which is the supreme object of all Catholic worship and thought. The apparitions at Lourdes in 1858 inspired great devotion and those unable to go there on pilgrimage erected Lourdes statues in their churches and held Marian devotions. When Pope Pius IX defined the doctrine of the Immaculate Conception in 1854 he was not expressing something new but proclaiming in formal and unmistakable terms what precisely was the teaching of the Church on the unique position of Our Blessed Lady. Likewise, when the decision was taken in 1847 to dedicate the church at Little Crosby under the ancient title of St. Mary, it was not something done by mere chance. Between 1829 and 1880 there were 44 churches in Lancashire and Cheshire alone dedicated to Our Lady under her various titles. Fr. Faber has already been mentioned as having given English Catholicism its unofficial national anthem. For Our Lady's birthday (a day surely ever memorable to all who love St. Mary's, Little Crosby) he wrote some lines that must often have been sung there: (29)

Dear Mother shall it always be that every passing year,
Shall make thee seem more beautiful, shall make thee grow more dear.
So close to God, so full of God dear Mother thou must be,
For ere the more we think of God the more we think of thee.

We knew thee to be free from stain as is the sun's bright beam,
We knew God's mother must be great, above what man could dream,
But Mary you are like the life the blessed lead above,
Unchangeable yet growing still in glory and in love.

The Catholic Revival

NOTES

(1) F. Tyrer, *History of R.C. Church of St. Mary, Little Crosby.* (Crosby Library C282 CRO. Typescript 1956).

(2) C.L. Lamb, *The Story of Crosby* (Crosby 1936) p37.

(3) F. Tyrer, *The Blundell of Crosby Family - A short Illustrated History* (Crosby 1960) pp41 - 42.

(4) H.N. Birt, *Obit Book of the English Benedictines 1600 - 1912* (Edinburgh 1913); *St. Mary's, Little Crosby: Parish Registers.*

(5) P. Hughes, *The Catholic Question* (London 1929) p253.

(6) Hughes pp306 - 311.

(7) F. Tyrer (Crosby Library C282 CRO).

(8) Tyrer.

(9) J. Gillow, *Bibliographical Dictionary of the English Catholics* 5 vols. (London 1885 - 1902) Vol 3, pp79 - 82.

(10) Tyrer.

(11) R.W. Church, *The Oxford Movement* (London 1891); E.S. Purcell, *Life of Cardinal Manning,* 2 vols. (London 1896); W. Ward, *The Life of John Henry Cardinal Newman,* 2 vols. (London 1913).

(12) R. Chapman, *Father Faber,* (London 1961).

(13) Tyrer.

(14) Tyrer.

(15) Tyrer.

(16) Birt; Crosby Library: Census Returns 1851 and 1861.

(17) Tyrer

(18) Tyrer

(19) Tyrer

(20) Crosby Library C282 STJ: *Sisters of Charity*

(21) *Catholic Encyclopaedia,* 15 vols. (New York 1908) Vol 3, pp 605 - 607.

(22) Crosby Library: *Sisters of Charity.*

(23) J.A. Hilton, *St. Joseph's Wrightington - A History* (Wigan 1994); Tyrer

(24) P. Doyle, 'Bishop Goss and the Gentry' in *North West Catholic History* Vol 12 (1985) pp6 - 13; J. Bennett, *Fr. Nugent of Liverpool* (Liverpool 1949).

(25) Tyrer.

(26) Crosby Hall: Archives.

(27) Crosby Library: *Sisters of Charity*; B. Plumb, *Found Worthy (Biographical Dictionary of the Secular Clergy of the Archdiocese of Liverpool)* (Warrington 1986).

(28) Tyrer

(29) Catholic Annual 1900; F.W. Faber, *Bethlehem* (London 1860); Faber, *Hymns* (Derby 1861).

CHAPTER 5

Wars, Laws and Renewal

"What is behind or ahead is less important than what is within."

Peter Byrne,
Keepers of Tomorrow, 1984.

At the dawn of the twentieth century Catholicism was very confident and assured. Duty towards God and neighbour was reflected in the devotional life of the Church and in the confraternities and social activities that it encouraged. Even when two terrible wars intervened the familiar round of the liturgical year and the character of the Church seemed by their very changelessness and stability to be a source of reassurance and consolation to many. For well over sixty years St. Mary's, Little Crosby knew only three parish priests. All were born and brought up in the nineteenth century, all were traditionalists in the finest sense of the word.

Two Canons

William Smith was born in Preston on 7 November, 1852 and educated at St. Edward's College, Liverpool and Ushaw. Ordained priest on 6 August, 1882, he taught at St. Edward's until 1889 when he was placed in charge of the new mission of All Saints, Anfield. In 1891 he moved to Sacred Heart, Ainsdale and in 1893 to St. Mary's, Little Crosby where he was to remain for twenty-nine years. He became a Canon in 1915. It appears that he was strong in frame but of somewhat diffident personality, likely to punctuate his sermons with hums and haws. Two notable administrative changes took place during his years. On 28 October, 1911, Liverpool was elevated to the rank of archdiocese with its fourth bishop, Thomas Whiteside, becoming first archbishop. On 12 November, 1918 all the existing Catholic missions in England were transformed into parishes.

Canon Smith

Ever since the restoration of the hierarchy in 1850 there had been, canonically speaking, no parish priests. They were often called rectors although their correct title (as anyone who has examined old baptismal registers knows) was Missionary

Apostolic, if in charge of a church, or Missionary Coadjutor if an assistant priest. The change was introduced and its implications explained in an *Ad Clerum* from the Archbishop, and parish priests with parochial rights were appointed, Canon Smith being among them. He died on 22 September, 1922 and is buried at Little Crosby. (1)

Canon Crook

John Crook was the son of John and Alice Crook, formerly Martland. He was born on 17 October, 1862 at Little Crosby where his father was coachman at the Hall. Educated at St. Edward's College, Liverpool and St. Joseph's College, Upholland, he was ordained priest on 4 June, 1887. He was curate at St. Michael's, Liverpool until 1890, at St. Joseph's, Anderton until 1891 and at St. Alexander's, Bootle until 1892. For the next thirty years he was in charge of St. Clare's, Sefton Park, a prosperous Liverpool parish renowned for its devotion to Mass and the Blessed Sacrament. In 1922 he was made honorary Canon and appointed to Little Crosby. His successor at St. Clare's was the newly consecrated auxiliary bishop, Robert Dobson. Canon Crook spent five years in his native parish where he wrote a very readable account of St. Edward's College as he had known it, fifty years before. In 1927 he was disturbed by an intruder in the presbytery and during the pursuit he caught a cold that developed into pneumonia from which he died on 15 October, 1927. He is buried at Little Crosby. (2)

Two Blundells

Trusts set up by Colonel Nicholas Blundell followed the usual pattern of the time giving the estate to his eldest son for life, followed by his children with sons preferred to daughters. His eldest son, William Joseph Blundell was born in 1851 and married in 1885 to Sicely, fourth daughter of Sir Humphrey de Trafford. But they had no children. He succeeded his father in 1894 and in the reminiscences of an 86 year old villager in 1978 he was "the finest man who ever lived." His interest in the parish seems to have been minimal, he devoted a lot of his time to amateur theatricals. He also kept numerous pets including a monkey. The gardens and woods were allowed to deteriorate. After his sudden death on 19 August, 1909, everything seemed to spring to life again with the advent of his successor and nephew, Francis Nicholas Blundell, the 28 year old son of the late Francis Nicholas (who died in 1884) and Mary, the novelist.

This new squire was born on 16 October, 1880, at *Altmouth*, Alt Road, Hightown, so he was less than four years old when his mother was widowed in April 1884.

He was educated at Stonyhurst and the Oratory School, Birmingham and Merton College, Oxford. He declined the presidency of the College Debating Society but, always an ardent Catholic, he became President of the Oxford Newman Society. He read for the Bar and went into chambers in Lincoln's Inn but a breakdown in health compelled him to spend a lengthy period in Switzerland, on Lake Como in Italy, where he helped to lay out a golf course at Dervio. After moving into Crosby Hall he set about improving the drainage of the land, built a pumping station and four cottages at Hightown and another four cottages at Little Crosby. He became a magistrate in 1910 and a county councillor in 1913. He also played a very active role in the Lancashire Farmers Association and was a member of the advisory committee on National Insurance, set up by Lloyd George in 1911. The future seemed bright with hope when, not for the first time, distant events resulted in massive conflict that not even Little Crosby was able to evade. (3)

World War 1

In 1914 Germany was much admired and greatly feared, though few would have admitted to the latter. Every visitor praised its industrial, municipal and social undertakings to such a degree that many Germans regarded themselves as members of a superior race. But, although it could and did trade freely with the rest of the world, having few colonies from which to obtain necessary raw materials, Germany felt somewhat deprived, perhaps inadequate. Certain outsiders went as far as saying Germany was looking for trouble. Its army, in which every able-bodied man was compelled to serve for a few years was its most venerated institution of all. Its very size was awesome.

In 1912 Germany had attempted (unsuccessfully) to obtain by treaty, Britain's neutrality in the event of a war with France. On 28 June, 1914 the Austrian Crown Prince Franz-Ferdinand and his wife were assassinated at Sarajevo. Their assassin was a Serb and at that time Serbia, although having a population of only five million, was an independent kingdom. Austria placed all the blame on Serbia and gave notice of impending retribution. At this, the Czar of Russia with whom the Serbs had much in common, both spiritually and culturally, told the Austrians not to be too severe on little Serbia. Events moved like wildfire. Germany warned Russia not to interfere in Austrian affairs and asked France to remain neutral in the event of war between Germany and Russia. France refused so Germany requested permission from Belgium for free passage of its armies across Belgian territory. This also was refused so Germany, with infamous barbarity that included sacking the University City of Louvain, invaded Belgium and advanced upon France. Britain, by an agreement of 1906, was pledged to provide a fighting force of 160,000 men in the event of such an attack, hence on 4 August, 1914 war was declared. (4)

Francis Blundell was commissioned in the Lancashire Hussars on 31 August, 1914. Many of the officers and men were Catholics and joined by other volunteers from

Little Crosby they all went under canvas at Knowsley. After various moves, to Canterbury where his sister Madge was a nurse in a military hospital, to Bisley and to Netheravon, he sailed for France on 9 November, 1915. His entire military career could be pieced together from his letters and journal. One letter which he wrote to his mother on Christmas Eve, 1915 must be included here.

"I am thinking of you all an extra lot tonight. Soon you will be going along to Midnight Mass, and I can see you walking up the church path, seeing the way quite well at first, then having a bit of a check where the path becomes black where the big beech tree used to stand, then feeling for the second gate and going rather uncertainly thro' the wood till you see the church spire standing up against the sky and come up to the wooden gate. Then as you go into the church, you will find that the light in the tribune is not lighted, but the lights in the body of the church are, and you will have the curious sense of looking thro' darkness into light. Probably Harry Wharton will be fussing about the crib and will open the door into the side chapel as you come in and will wish you a merry Xmas in the gloomiest of tones. Then the altar boys will come in and make feverish efforts to light the candles and will probably set some of the decorations on fire. Then Mass will begin and Fr. Smith will look very clean and big compared with the altar boys and there will be a sort of rustle thro' the church as people kneel down and Fr. Smith will hum and haw a bit after the Gospel. Then the solemn part will come and the time will fly by in a second or two, as it seems, till the Holy Communion begins and you will have row after row of good ugly Little Crosby faces coming up to the rails with that splendid look of reverence inborn from generations of Catholic forefathers and they will all genuflect and make the sign of the cross before they come away from the rails. To me it is always one of the most beautiful moments of the year to see them all rolling up on Xmas night, with all their jealousies and dislikes and meanesses and pettinesses forgotten and only thinking of Xmas and of all it means. Then you will come back through the dark wood and when you come to the first iron gate you will see the lights shining and welcoming you and when you come up to the door you will find Slaytor waiting for you with a subdued joy and an uncomprehending pleasure in your holiness, which he feels and appreciates but cannot understand. Then you will pass through that puzzling phase when you are divided between holiness and worldliness over the mutton broth and then go peacefully to bed. I am crying like anything as I write this. I am with you all in spirit all the time and feeling Little Crosby in my bones and loving and appreciating its faith." (5)

Francis was gazetted captain in December 1916, dated back to 31 July. Despite active service at Passchendaele and on the Somme he survived unscathed, but only just. His best friend Micky Rawstorne was killed by a shell as they stood side by side. In 1918 he became Aide-de-camp to General Sir Aylmer Hunter-Watson. Five Little Crosby men gave their lives in that war and their names are inscribed on the parish war memorial, designed by Mellard Reade.

Joseph Bristow,	Royal Army Service Corps
John Orme,	7th Kings Liverpool Regiment
James Rainford,	7th Kings Liverpool Regiment
Joseph Rainford,	2nd battalion 5th Lancashire Fusiliers
William Rimmer,	8th Kings Liverpool Regiment

Marriage

On 11 April, 1918, Francis became engaged to Theresa Victoria Ward, of Dorking. They had met while she was working in a recreation centre, organised by the Catholic Womens League, at Boulogne. Her father, Wilfrid Ward, was biographer of Cardinals Newman and Wiseman, and benefactor of numerous good causes. *The Tablet* once described the Wards as one of the families that had helped to shape English Catholic history. Theresa's mother, the former Josephine Hope-Scott, was grand-daughter of the 14th Duke of Norfolk. The wedding took place on 25 July, 1918, at Brompton Oratory, with Nuptial Mass celebrated by the bride's uncle, Bishop Ward of Brentwood. (6)

Parliament

As early as 1917 Francis was regarded as a suitable prospective Member of Parliament when the old Waterloo constituency was looking for a candidate. Objections on the grounds of his religion had been raised but disregarded because he seemed well fitted for such a position, but nothing came of it. On 15 November, 1922, he was elected Conservative Member for the Ormskirk Division of Lancashire by 11,921 and a majority of 3,547 over his Labour rival. His speeches and questions were mostly confined to agricultural and farming interests but he opposed a Bill to allow easier divorce, remarking "The House can make women bear arms but it cannot make men bear babies."

He was re-elected in 1923 when one of the current promises was a minimum wage of thirty shillings (£1.50p) a week for farm workers. He continued to ask searching questions. For example it was illegal to sell seed potatoes that did not comply with agricultural certification but any prosecution had to be instigated within six months of purchase. But as it took more than six months for the crops to grow and any irregularity be detected, he wanted to know how could any prosecutions possibly take place. A written reply, to another question, filled eight pages of Hansard. However in 1924 he raised a question that might easily fill a hundred or more pages of Catholic history. (7)

The Roman Catholic Relief Act of 1926

In 1924 the population of the Scottish village of Carfin, near Motherwell was three-quarters Catholic. Every year on the feast of Corpus Christi they held an outdoor procession. Its fame spread far and in 1923 an estimated 50,000 persons took part. The 1924 procession was announced for 22 June but a few days earlier the local police Superintendent told the parish priest that any priests participating would be indicted under the Catholic Emancipation Act of 1829. The Chief Constable reiterated this but said the procession presented traffic difficulties, adding that if the priest allowed the procession to take place he would be reported to the Crown Authorities. So it was restricted to the church grounds.

Francis Nicholas Blundell

On 2 July and again on 8 July, Francis raised the matter in the House of Commons and was told by the Secretary of State for Scotland that it was a case of obstructing a public thoroughfare. Francis was not satisfied with the reply and said the Catholic Emancipation Act had been invoked which had nothing to do with traffic control. He insisted that it was not a question of traffic but whether or not obsolete law was to be invoked against certain of His Majesty's subjects. It transpired that no higher authority had given orders to the Police but action had been taken after a complaint by a common informer. On 23 July the Prime Minister declined to make time available to facilitate a Bill to remove such disabilities but Francis Blundell would not relent.

There followed some anti-Catholic and anti-Irish speeches in the House and a few people wrote to newspapers saying they would not have voted for Francis had they known he would pursue such a matter. This led, on 4 August, to one of his most impassioned speeches: "I stand here as a Catholic of Catholics but I have been sent here by 30,000 of my fellow citizens, not more than one eighth of them belong to my religion. That is the spirit of the present time. In the 16th and 17th centuries two of my forefathers died in prison and one was born in prison, for their devotion to the Catholic faith.........I do appeal that the Government will support the Bill I am introducing to remove these disabilities once and for all from the Statute Book." (8)

Before any further progress was made Francis had been made a Deputy Lieutenant for Lancashire and (on 29 October, 1924) re-elected for Ormskirk. It must be understood that objections to the procession at Carfin rested upon a clause in the 1829 Emancipation Act that forbade a priest or religious to appear in public wearing a habit or vestments. It was also disputed whether or not a procession was a rite or ceremony of the Roman Catholic Church. But Francis had discovered other laws, extant if not applied, that could also impose disabilities upon Catholics. There were nineteen of them.

1. An Act of 1549 forbidding books of Roman Catholic ritual ever to be kept in this realm.

2. An Act of 1559 making any gift to a religious order void and superstitious.

3. An Act of 1715 declaring gifts to convents or monasteries to be void.

4. An Act of 1737 which prevented a Catholic from leaving an advowson to his family or from giving it away.

5. Part of the 1791 Relief Act which forbade a priest to officiate in a building with a bell or steeple attached to it.

6. Part of the same Act forbidding Catholic societies to be formed.

7. Part of the Catholic Emancipation Act of 1829 which imposed a fine of £50 on any priest or religious who wore a habit outside a church or private house, or exercised Catholic rites outside a church or private house.

8. Part of the same Act requiring members of religious orders to register with a Clerk of the Peace or forfeit £50 a month for failing to do so.

9. Part of the same Act which stated members of religious orders coming into this country could be banished for life.

10. Part of the same Act which permitted the return of one so banished provided they register.

11. Part of the same Act which provided the Secretary of State to grant licences to remain for six months.

12. Part of the same Act which provided for annual returns of such licences.

13. Part of the same Act which stated any person admitting another to membership of a religious order be guilty of a misdemeanour.

14. Part of the same Act which permitted any so admitted to be banished for life.

15. Part of the same Act which permitted deportation of any such person not leaving within thirty days.

16. Part of the same Act which stated that any banished person who had not left within three months should be transported for life.

17. Section 4 of the R.C. Charities Act of 1832 which continued disabilities against religious orders.

18. Section 15 of an Act of 1844 similar to the above.

19. Section 7 of the R.C. Charities Act of 1860 which continued the above disabilities. (9)

The Bill was introduced into the House on 10 March, 1926 by the Member for Watford, Dennis Herbert who was not a Catholic, under the ten minute rule. He stressed that it was aimed solely at removing penalties from Catholics and in no way sought to affect the rights of succession to the throne or the legal position of the Church of England. It received considerable support from Anglicans, Free Churchmen and Jews, also some colourful if not always accurate hostility. By far the greatest objections were those against the Host being carried in public. A Northern Ireland Member who proposed that the Bill should not apply there had to be informed that the Government of Ireland Act of 1920 had already removed such disabilities, but he still objected to it being applied to the rest of the British Isles. A move to prevent it applying to Scotland was defeated by 200 votes to 22. Vigorous opposition from outside Parliament came from the Anglican Bishop of Manchester, Dr. Knox, who said he blamed Berlin for the Great War, Moscow for the General Strike and the Vatican for the current preoccupation with Popery. He added that danger to the spirit being greater than danger to the body this last was the worst of them all. Numerous other alliances and Orange Lodges also voiced objections.

When the Bill returned to the House on 3 December, 1926, twenty-nine members spoke, not all of them sympathetically. There were still people who thought all members of religious orders must inevitably be foreigners! No Member was willing to act as teller for the Noes so the Bill was passed and sent to the House of Lords. There, on 10 December, 1926 it was introduced by Viscount FitzAlan of Derwent who received support from the Archbishop of Canterbury. On 14 December, Earl Russell could not forbear to remark, "I hope the noble Viscount will repeat the advantages of toleration when we come to consider such questions as divorce or birth control." But he did not oppose the Bill which was passed and received the Royal Assent on the following day.

At Carfin they held a celebratory torchlight procession and a new railway station was built to accommodate even more visitors. The Archbishop of Liverpool and the Anglican Archdeacon of Liverpool both warmly congratulated Francis. Cardinal Bourne, writing on behalf of the Pope as well as himself, sent special medals to him and Mr. Herbert. But a section of the Ormskirk Conservative Association was anything but pleased. (10)

Fr. Holden

Fr. Holden

After Canon Crook's death Fr. Thomas Holden was appointed parish priest. He was born in Preston on 25 September, 1885, educated at Ushaw and ordained on 21 January, 1912. After twelve years as curate at St. Mary's, Chorley, illness compelled him to spend three years at Teignmouth, Devon. On recovery he was sent to Little Crosby to see if the place agreed with him. It must have done as he remained for twenty-six years. He was an excellent preacher and although few people had cars at the time, many travelled long distances just to listen to him.

On Sunday and Monday, 25 and 26 August, 1929, the centenary of Catholic Emancipation was celebrated. The Rector of Stonyhurst, Fr. Walter Weld, S.J., preached at solemn High Mass in the morning. In the afternoon there was a procession of the Blessed Sacrament with Benediction in the woods and again in front of Crosby Hall. On Monday there were sporting events all day for the children, and in the evening dancing on the lawns ending at nine o'clock with the National Anthem.

In 1937 Fr. Holden's priestly silver jubilee was honoured with the presentation of a spiritual bouquet and the school and church choir combining to perform the music-drama The Wreck of the Argosy. In 1953 he retired to Brinscall Hall, a convent of the Canonesses of St. Augustine, where he died on 22 February, 1960 but was buried at Little Crosby. (11)

The English Martyrs Chapel

The approach of the centenary of Catholic Emancipation revived great interest in the sufferings of the martyrs of the 16th and 17th centuries. In December 1929 Pope Pius XI beatified one hundred and thirty-six of them and the cause of two - John Fisher and Thomas More - proceeded towards canonisation which was achieved in 1935. All this prompted Francis to have the chapel originally erected as a memorial to his father in 1887 to be re-decorated and designated as the English Martyrs Chapel. The frescoes were designed and painted by George Arthur

Tomlinson, who later became a Monsignor and administrator of Westminster Cathedral. But at that time he was a seminarist in Rome who spent his holidays with the Wyse family of Waterloo. It was during these periods that his work at Little Crosby was accomplished.

The Panels depict (1) St. Thomas More at his Chelsea home. (2) St. John Fisher on the scaffold. (3) Blessed Laurence Johnson celebrating Mass in the Oak Room of Crosby Hall. (4) Blessed Richard Hurst, a Lancashire martyr arrested while ploughing. (5) Blessed John Rigby on a hurdle. (6) Blessed Richard Langhorne, friend of William Blundell the Cavalier, and victim of the Titus Oates conspiracy. (7) Blundell family at prayer. (8) St. Edmund Arrowsmith as a boy. (9) Blessed Richard Wrenno, a Chorley weaver. The coats of arms are (1) Richard Blundell who died in prison at Lancaster. (2) William Blundell the Recusant. (3) William Blundell the Cavalier. (4) William Joseph Blundell, founder of St. Mary's, Little Crosby. (5) Colonel Nicholas Blundell who died in 1894. (6) Arrowsmith. (7) Johnson. (8) Fisher and More. (9) Langhorne. (10) Rigby. (11) Richard Blundell (1929 - 1936). (12) Francis Nicholas Blundell who instigated all this artwork. (12)

The English Martyrs Chapel

Death of Francis Nicholas Blundell

Ironically the Chapel of the English Martyrs became Francis Blundell's memorial, a panel on the wall telling us that he died on 28 October, 1936. He was defeated at Ormskirk at the General Election of 1929 but in 1930 the Preston Conservatives invited him to become their candidate. This was graciously declined, one reason being that as Chairman of the Catholic Education Council he did not wish to convey any idea that his Parliamentary position might be used to favour Catholic Schools, which were the burning issue of those decades. Francis was unwell throughout most of the year 1936 and the

The Village Memorial to Francis Nicholas Blundell

death of his youngest son, Richard, on 1 March was a severe blow. But he rallied his strength and on the feast of Christ the King, only three days before his death, he spoke at a huge meeting in St. George's Hall, Liverpool at the request of Archbishop Downey. He died in London where he had gone to attend a family wedding and the funeral took place at Little Crosby on 30 October. Among several newspaper tributes it is stated "His relations with his people were as nearly perfect as such human relations can be." Had he lived he would have become the first Mayor of the new Borough of Crosby in 1937. The local people erected a commemorative wayside crucifix, only a stonesthrow from the historic Ned Howard's Cottage. (13) In dedicating the second volume of the trilogy *Old Catholic Lancashire*, his cousin, Fr. Frederick Odo Blundell, O.S.B., wrote:

To the Memory of
Francis Nicholas Blundell
Squire of Little Crosby
Born October 16, 1880, died October 28, 1936
Privy Chamberlain to His Holiness
Justice of the Peace and Deputy Lieutenant for Lancashire
Member of Parliament for Ormskirk Division 1922 -1929
Promoter of the Catholic Relief Bill, 1926
Member of Lancashire County Council, 1913 - 1936
President of the Lancashire Farmers Association
Captain, Lancashire Hussars Yeomanry, 1914 - 1919
Member of the Empire Marketing Board
Chairman of the Parliamentary Poultry Commission and
Member of the Parliamentary Milk Commission
Chairman of the Catholic Education Council
A worthy and devoted son of Catholic Lancashire

World War 2

The defeat inflicted upon Germany in 1918 went ill indeed with so proud a race of people. But the subsequent folly of the Allies made an easy path for the dictatorship of Hitler. Never one to mince words, he defiantly proclaimed "So long as Germany does not fend for herself no one else will. Her lost provinces cannot be regained by solemn appeals to heaven or the League of Nations but only by force of arms. Nothing can be effected by the bourgeois virtues of peace and order." Thus on 3 September 1939 Britain found itself at war with Germany again. Crosby Hall became a Red Cross hospital with accommodation for forty to fifty patients. It was staffed by the Misses Madge and Agnes Blundell and a number of local people, one of whom, Miss Teresa Jones, still lives in the village. Bombs fell at

Hightown, in the Mill Field and in the woods near Oaklands Cottage, but there were no casualties. (14)

Strict blackout regulations prevented the Christmas Midnight Mass and all church bells were silenced for the duration of the war because their ringing was to be the signal of an enemy invasion. Even palms could no longer be imported so permission was given for locally grown willow to be distributed on Palm Sunday. Fasting and abstinence was abolished and while restored in 1949 it never quite achieved its ancient stature and became voluntary in 1968. Eventually two names were inscribed on the parish War Memorial: Francis Jackson, of the Royal Navy, whose mother was a Heptonstall and lived next to Heatherlea Farm, and Signalman Joseph Lupton of Delph Road whose father worked a threshing machine. (15)

Church Centenary

On Saturday, 23 August 1947 a garden party and dance took place in the grounds of Crosby Hall at which the band of St. Edward's Orphanage, Broadgreen performed. A commemorative article, mostly culled from Old Catholic Lancashire and photograph appeared in the Cathedral Record, which was then the monthly journal of the Archdiocese of Liverpool. But redecoration of the church and the repair of a large crack that had appeared in the wall of the Martyrs chapel had to wait until 1955. (16)

On 30 September 1949, Nicholas Blundell died at the early age of 24. He inherited the estate on the death of his father in 1936, was educated at Ampleforth and Christ Church, Oxford, and went to visit America after passing his Bar finals. Regrettably he caught poliomyelitis and died soon after his return to England. Nicholas lies buried among his ancestors, just outside the east window of St. Mary's. The estate then passed to his sister, the present Mrs. Hester Mary Whitlock Blundell. (17)

"The finest part of England"

Fr. Anderton

When Fr. Holden retired in 1953, Liverpool was awaiting the appointment of a new Archbishop, so the Vicar Capitular asked Fr. Thomas Marsh, chaplain at Notre Dame Convent, Birkdale, to look after St. Mary's until a permanent appointment could be made. Some say Fr. Marsh did not care very much for country life and was glad to move on to St. Benedict's, Hindley, early in 1954. But the next parish priest, himself a countryman loved country ways. Fr. Lawrence Anderton was born at Anderton, near Chorley in 1901 and educated at St. Edward's College, Liverpool and Oscott College, Birmingham. Ordained priest on 25 May, 1929, he held several curacies, notably at St. Robert Bellarmine and St. Monica's, Bootle, Mount Carmel, Liverpool and Our Lady's, Formby. In the terrible May blitz of 1941 he was blown from one Bootle street to another and sustained two broken legs. His love of skating caused a few other injuries. In October, 1944 he became parish priest of St. Peter's Woolston and from 1946 until moving to Little Crosby in February 1954, he was parish priest of Our Lady of Lourdes, Birkdale. For twenty years he was devoted to Little Crosby and its traditions. While instructing the children he said on several occasions "You may not realise it but you are living in the finest part of England." Not that he was anything of a recluse, as he loved fishing and often took a holiday in Ireland where he was welcomed by the Benedictine nuns at Kylemore, Co. Galway. His articles on *Lough Derg* and *Around Kylemore* were published in the *Cathedral Record*. (18)

The Second Vatican Council

In 1960 Pope John XXIII announced a General Council of the Church, the twenty-first such event in its entire history. The stated aims were to "Bring back those who are distant, gather in those who are scattered and call to life those who are dead to grace." Missionaries from Africa and Asia and prelates from Communist-dominated parts of Europe, where preaching and teaching being forbidden the liturgy was the only means of imparting faith, convinced the Council of the need for Mass and the Sacraments to be performed in the vernacular. So Latin ceased to be the universal language of the Church. English people learned that the Protestant Reformation of the 16th century was but one of a number of schisms reaching from Nestorian and Monophysite separations in the 5th century to the split between Catholic and Orthodox Christianity in the 11th. So no longer were we to pray for our separated brethren to return to the one true fold, but for the return of the unity and peace for which Christ prayed. The Pope said he wanted to alter Catholic attitudes not the Catholic faith, but some *Periti* (advisers) in denouncing Triumphalism as being out of date with the social attitudes and expectations of the twentieth century led some extremists to make claims that the Council had not even envisaged let alone sanctioned. These people led an onslaught on solemnity and tradition, in the mistaken idea that it would promote Christian unity. Even the position of Our Lady was assailed.

A whole book could be written about those who left the priesthood, the religious life and the Church itself, but it would simply be an account of history repeating itself, because every General Council has left some group or other thoroughly dissatisfied. But all the rest, St. Mary's, Little Crosby included, were left to implementing the real intentions of the Council. Any change here was relatively painless and mostly executed after Fr. Anderton's death on 10 August, 1975. (19)

The School

In 1842, years before the Government ever dreamed of providing education for the nation's children, there were 236 Catholic schools in England, 33 of them in London. In that year Squire William Blundell took the first step towards providing one at Little Crosby. Sited near the Great Crosby boundary, it was a single storey construction of local stone measuring 50 feet by 30feet, with a screen dividing it into two rooms. When it opened on 6 November, 1843, the hundred children (who included some from Great Crosby and Hightown) were treated to buns, rice pudding and negus, that is wine diluted with hot water and spiced with sugar etc. Mr. Blundell acted as manager and inspector, and for a time two of his daughters, Catherine and Frances, taught there. A little later the names of Mr. Craven and Mr. Sherlock appear as masters. As well as raising financial support by concerts and raffles, and the collection of school pence - a system that survived into the twentieth century - the proceeds of other social events went to support the newly opened Catholic Blind Asylum in Liverpool. The curriculum consisted of reading, writing, arithmetic, needlework, painting and singing, but it is recorded that from the age of eight, most children were expected to work on the farms and only attended school in the depths of winter when there was nothing else for them to do.

Crosby Hall circa 1965

When the arrival of the Sisters of Charity was expected, Squire Nicholas Blundell, who had succeeded his father in 1854, was prompted to provide better accommodation. What remained of the old church at West Lane House was made available and a new school and convent erected on the site. Hadfield, the architect of the church, drew up plans and local labour completed the building by 17 December, 1858. The nuns came the following June and the pattern of schooling was established that was to endure to well within living memory. The first mention of an external religious examination was in 1885. Before then the local priest performed that task and there are grounds for believing that methods pioneered here were later recommended elsewhere.

In 1870 after a lot of debate the Government succeeded in passing an Act to make elementary education available to all, though it was not made compulsory until 1880. The Act was surrounded by controversy because of the differences of contending parties. Broadly speaking, Anglicans, Catholics and Jews were willing to cooperate in return for support from the Treasury. But there was a proportion of secularists, often aided and abetted by the Nonconformists who fought tooth and nail to exclude all religious teaching from education and placed obstacles innumerable in the path of those who opposed them. For example, if a school was surrendered to the state system it received a subsidy of one pound per place while those that were not surrendered received only seven shillings (35p). It was this very climate that ensured the school at Little Crosby remaining beyond public funding, and therefore beyond unsympathetic reach, until 1921, by which time much of the old bitterness had gone. After some just criticism Canon Bennett appealed to Paris for more efficient nuns to improve standards. Sister Clare Quigley was one of those sent and she remained from 1879 until 1919, still remembered by one or two of the older parishioners. Another was Sister Teresa Parker whose expertise at producing costumes for concerts and plays from almost nothing was long remembered. (20)

In 1876 the school leaving age was fixed at the age of ten. In 1893 it was raised to eleven, in 1899 to twelve and in 1918 to fourteen. In 1939 it was extended to fifteen but because of the war suspended until 1947. The school at Little Crosby, despite having only two classrooms, known affectionately as the little school and the big school, kept pace with these requirements and remained an all age school until 1954 when the senior children transferred to St. Bede's at Great Crosby. The first lay staff were engaged about 1930; Miss Alty and Miss Russell and later Miss Hiddleston and Miss Pennington who both taught in the old school and the present one. Sister Margaret who was here from 1947 until 1970 was the last head of the old school.

When Fr. Anderton became parish priest in 1954 he recognised that a new school was an immediate necessity. Some say he was a distant relative of Sir Francis Robert Ince Anderton (1859- 1950) of Euxton Hall, Chorley, whose generosity had left a trust fund to which worthy causes might apply. By doing so part of the money required to build the new school which was designed by Messrs. Lionel Prichard and Son and built by T. Sloyan and Sons, of Liverpool, was obtained. It was first occupied in 1963 having taken eighteen months to build. Mrs. Mary

Claire Barnes became head teacher in 1970. That same year the Sisters of Charity of St. Vincent de Paul left Little Crosby after an association of over 110 years. From 1973 until 1994 the convent was occupied by Franciscan Missionaries of Mill Hill, two of whom - Sisters Moira and Immaculata - taught in the school for brief periods.

Numbers attending have varied from 50 in 1963 to around 85 in 1980. Then with a decrease to 26 in 1990 there was a real danger of closure. But it survived, numbers rocketed to 101 and in 1994 an extra classroom, a mobile one formerly belonging to Holy Rosary, Old Roan, was obtained and named 'St. Anthony's'. While this was in transit the old school was used again for a few terms, but that has now become a private house.

With its badge, centred by the red rose of Lancashire and quartered with the figure of Our Lady, the Blundell Arms, the village and the sea, St. Mary's is a traditional Catholic school. First Communion, May procession, Blessed Sacrament procession through the woods, Harvest Festival in September and nativity play at Christmas fill out the time-honoured pattern. And through the year every day at noon one of the older children goes across to the church to ring the Angelus. In March 1997 Mrs. Mary Claire Barnes, head teacher was assisted by Mesdames Colette Pope, Jane Tumilty, Moyra Williams, Patricia Davies and Maria Williams. At that time the school was at the centre of the much publicised OFSTED Report which found "A good school whose excellent ethos reflects a good caring relationship. Very well managed, efficient and effective. Is very good value for money." (21)

Claire Barnes, Head Teacher
Repainted the Litany in 1997

More Benedictines

Between 1977 and 1982 there was a brief return of the Benedictines to the village when a small group of Ampleforth monks moved into the Barn House at Crosby Hall. The intention was to complement the works of parishes and schools and provide people with space to respond to current issues of Justice and Peace and social environment. The work continues over at Ince Blundell and has been described as being to Liverpool a little of what Bethany was to Jerusalem. (22)

Crosby Hall Educational Trust (CHET)

This was set up by Christopher David (who had set up something similar near Bristol) and Mark Blundell, between 1988 and 1991 and involved the raising of £900,000. It is a residential educational centre occupying the historic stables and farm buildings at Crosby Hall. It was opened by Her Royal Highness The Princess Margaret on 8 May, 1991. Here children are introduced to trees, fields, flowers, animals and the countryside generally. One aim is to make the facilities available to children and young people regardless of handicap or ability to pay. Provision is made for the disabled. There are walks in the woods and grounds of the estate, and facilities to study the history, geography, biology, botany and farming of the area. Other resources are provided at the Coastguard Station, the sand dunes and the seashore. A Confidence Course contains a high level Burma Bridge, chain bridge, rope ladders, slide and obstacles. The centre also provides table tennis, draughts, chess. Older students and adults are welcomed and organisations may run their own courses, and day courses can be provided even when a school is in residence. Art, photography, dance, drama, basketry, pottery, spinning, batik, collage, bird watching and astronomy are also offered. (23)

Mgr. Breen meets the Pope

Two Monsignori

After the death of Fr. Anderton it was announced that Canon Francis Kiernan, who had just retired as head master of the Cardinal Allen Grammar School at West Derby was to be the new parish priest. But after a brief visit he decided not to remain. Having been a military chaplain in the second world war and used to a very busy professional life for a further twenty years, Little Crosby seemed too somnolent a prospect. The parish by then contained no more than the village. Hightown had been independent since 1929, its church of Our Lady of Victories built on land donated by F.N. Blundell in 1916. Thornton was transferred to the parish of St. William of York in 1955. So the next parish priest was Monsignor Sidney Breen, a native of Liverpool, ordained at Upholland on 18 May, 1940. After a short time at St. Oswald's, Ashton in Makerfield, Mgr. Breen spent 29 years at Upholland College. He was Prefect of Discipline, Professor of Philosophy, Procurator - and from 1958 until 1972 - Rector. Then followed three years as parish

Mgr. Rigby

priest of St. Paul's West Derby before his appointment to Little Crosby. He explained that having just organised the reordering of the church at West Derby he was in no hurry to repeat such an undertaking. But he offered some words as to why, in the light of current liturgical development, such a thing ought to be considered. The idea was achieved by nothing being actually removed from the church. A few items were resited and the baptismal font from old St. Augustine's, Liverpool was obtained and placed to the right of the entrance to the Sanctuary. Its stone is almost identical to that of St. Mary's and its size more suited to the prominence now given to that Sacrament. The altar rails were placed against the chancel walls and the altar from the Martyr's chapel brought out to face the congregation. The former baptistery became a shrine of Our Lady and the organ in the gallery was moved sidewards, a move that allowed much more light to penetrate the large west window. The tabernacle from the High Altar was moved to the Martyr's chapel although the Blessed Sacrament remains reserved on the High Altar, a smaller tabernacle having been placed there. The Pieta now to be seen near the entrance to this chapel was formerly in the presbytery.

Memorials to various deceased members of the Blundell family were re-sited in the family tribune. These include one to Osbert Joseph, uncle of F.N. Blundell, M.P., and another to Louise Blundell Uzovics, widow of Captain Charles Blundell (1818 - 1895) third son of the Founder. She died at Petheofalva in her native Hungary, on 2 January, 1913. Apart from a very ancient picture the tribune also contains memorials to Margaret and Agnes Blundell, daughters of Mrs. Blundell the authoress, and brasses to Mary and Emily Teresa Blundell, daughters of the Founder, who became nuns, and William, his second son, killed in Rangoon in 1852.

In 1992 following a severe fall, Mgr. Breen decided to retire to nearby Thornton, where at the time of writing he remains, ever genial and welcoming my several enquiries. At St. Mary's, his successor was Mgr. James Judge Rigby, who came from St. Thomas of Canterbury, Waterloo. Very conscious of the place Little Crosby occupies in English Catholic history and very proud to be considered worthy of such an appointment, Mgr. Rigby had great ideas for the parish when, less than a year in office, he suffered a thrombosis and died on 17 December, 1992 at the age of 65. A musician, a journalist and a member of the Archdiocesan Liturgical Commission, Mgr. Rigby, a native of Wigan, had been a Prelate of Honour to the Pope since 1980. Formerly of St. James's, Bootle, St. George's, Maghull, St. Helen's, Crosby and St. John's, Kirkdale, he was parish priest of St. Luke's, Whiston for about one year, 1978 - 1979. His grave is in the new extension of St. Mary's cemetery, first used in 1973. (24)

Memoirs and Memorabilia

Moving among the parishioners has, not surprisingly, caused recall of persons and events past and present. One told of Canon Smith as being very benevolent. In days before the National Health Service or Social Security there were times when he even paid for funerals. The old school belfry, so prominent in the illustration in *Old Catholic Lancashire*, becoming dangerous was taken down in 1926. The cemetery, gardens and greenhouses were faithfully tended for years by John Makin, and by John Fleetwood before him. Until 1947 there was a Tontine that for a modest sum per week provided payment in sickness or at death, and a club supper every winter. John Jones, and later two of his sons, attended to all the Christmas and Harvest decorations for over a hundred years. Teresa Jones looked after the annual Corpus Christi altar for fifty years. One parishioner possesses a picture of F.N. Blundell with a medal sent to him by the Pope. Another remembers Belgian refugees coming to the village in World War 1. Yet another mentioned that although there are three riding schools in the area there are no longer any working farm horses. More than one told of a visitor mistaking Fr. Anderton for a beggar and giving him money, others expressed appreciation of the Parish Hall (the former Club House) used for Bingo, wedding receptions, refreshments after funerals, and for fund-raising events.

Several of the nuns served as organists as did Mrs. Margaret Wright, formerly Massam, and Miss Joan Rainford. Tributes were paid to Miss June Houlmann, the present organist and to Mollie Gilligan, sacristan for upwards of thirty years. And on no account must we omit Fr. Francis O'Leary, the Mill Hill priest born at 22, The Village, Little Crosby, founder of Jospice International and once the subject of the television programme *This is your life*. (25)

Canon Daley and his People

Early in 1993 Canon Roger Austin Daley became parish priest. He was born in Liverpool in 1931 and educated at St. Francis Xavier's College and Liverpool University where he graduated in Law. After being an articled clerk and qualifying as a solicitor, he entered the Venerable English College in Rome and was ordained priest on 29 October, 1961. A brief spell at St. Teresa's, Birkdale preceded his return to Rome and a further degree in Canon Law. When he returned to Liverpool he was given special responsibilities at the Curial Offices, mostly in the Matrimonial Tribunal. But these have always been combined with parochial or chaplaincy duties. Over the past thirty years Canon

Canon Daley

Daley has served St. Alban's, Athol Street, Liverpool, the old pro-cathedral of St. Nicholas, All Saints, Anfield, St. Hugh of Lincoln, Liverpool, where he was in charge for a few years. He then became chaplain to the Good Shepherd Convent, Wavertree and was created honorary Canon in 1990. In anticipation of the 150th anniversary of the church a slide show and exhibition are being arranged and probably some marquee events.

While remembering that those recusants of old had their names taken as a means of punishment and degradation, the present day congregation wishing to be associated willingly and lovingly with everything that St. Mary's, Little Crosby represents, was invited, on Sunday, 12 April, 1997, to have their names taken. Two hundred and eighty-one people responded.

Thomas Ronald Aindow
Desmond Aldridge
Steven Aldridge
John Ashcroft
Maria Ashcroft
Peter Ashcroft
Jennifer Atcheson
Peter Atcheson

Mary Agnes Aindow
Sybil Aldridge
Annette Aldridge
Brenda Ashcroft
Patricia Ashcroft
Barbara Atcheson (nee Blundell)
Rachel Atcheson

Joseph Barnes
Mary Anne Barnes
Irene Blundell
Elaine Blundell
Katie Blundell
Charles Bold
Gillian Breen
David Brownrigg
James Brownrigg

Mary Claire Barnes
David Blundell
Paul Blundell
Michaela Blundell
Marcia Boffey
Paul Breen
Anthony Breen
Pauline Brownrigg
Michael Brownrigg

John Cahill
Christopher Cahill
John Cahill
Irene Cadley
Kerry Clarke
Mary Clulee
Patricia Cosser
Margaret Costigan
Norman William Cresswell
Nicholas Cresswell
Francis Crowley

Marie Cahill
Laura Cahill
Maureen Cahill
Charles Clarke
Thomas Clulee
Denis Cosser
Michael Cosser
Martha Patricia Cox
Mary Cresswell
Mark Cresswell
Sheila Crowley

John Dahill
Doris D'Arcy
Yvonne Della Corte
David Delve
Peter Delve
Lelia Donnelly
William Dutton

Philomena Dahill
Nicola Della Corte
Susan Delve
Janet Delve
Vincent Donnelly
Patricia Doyle
Mary Dutton

Michael Eddy
Bernard Elliott

Helen Eddy

Lillian Frankham
Simone Frankham

Yvonne Frankham
Gordon Frankham

Oonagh M. Gallagher
Thomas Garrett
Catherine Gaskell (nee Kehlenbeck)
Gillian Marie Gaskell)
Michael Gaskell   )
Maureen Gilbertson
Mollie Gilligan
Elizabeth Goodwin

Catherine Garner
Gerard Gaskell

(believed to be the first Gaskells
to originate from Little Crosby)
Paul Gilbertson
Christopher Gilligan
Mary Gray

Peter Hall
Joan Harrington
Michael Joseph Harris
Catherine Hickey
Monica Patricia Hopkins
John Hulligan
June Houlmann

Joan Hall
Bartholomew Harrington (R.I.P.)
Eileen Mary Harris (nee Beglin)
James Christopher Hopkins
Christopher James Hopkins
Jean Hulligan

Brian Jones
Ita Jones
Matthew Jones
Teresa Jones

George Henry Jones
Jane Jones (nee Wright)
Margaret Jones

Douglas Francis Kane
Frederick Kehlenbeck
Susan Kemp (nee Breen)

Sandra Ann Kane
Josephine Kehlenbeck (nee Gilbertson)
Richard Kemp

Rose Kemp
Ann Kerwin
Teresa Kiernan
Raymond Kiernan

Joseph Kerwin
Gordon Alfred Kidman
Pauline Kiernan

Norman Larkin
Francis Larkin
Anthony Larkin
Derek Leadbetter
Mary Lochhead
Marjorie Lupton
Bernard Lupton
Sally Lupton
Thomas Lupton

Mary Larkin (nee Makin)
Cecilia Larkin
Martin Larkin
Margaret Leadbetter
George Lupton senior
George Lupton junior
Lynne Lupton
John Lupton

William Ronald McCartney
Tony McClure
Terence McKenna
Victoria McKenna
Alex McNeill
Helen Mahon
Henry Joseph Makin (R.I.P.)
Margaret Makin
James Mann
Dorothy Massam (R.I.P.)
Esther Matthews
Catherine Moya Milsom
Victoria Jane Milsom
Denis G. Murphy

Rosanne McCartney (nee Bristow)
Luke McGuinness
Brenda Ann McKenna
Rebecca McKenna
Kitty McNeill
Mary Agnes Makin
Stephen Makin
Bernadette Makin
Robert J. Massam (R.I.P.)
Ronald Matthews
Jennifer Matthews
Catherine Shelley Milsom
David Edward Milsom
Patricia M. Murphy

Michael Orme
Norah M. O'Rourke

Francis O'Rourke

Barrie Partington
Clare Partington
Christopher Payne
Elizabeth Patricia Penlington
Mark Pennington
Richard Pennington
Colette Pope
Linda Pope

Joan Partington
Victoria Partington
John Richardson Penlington
Geraldine Penlington
Diane Pennington
Katie Pennington
Colin Pope
James Pope

Andrew Pope
Dorothy Pope
Pamela Pope
Stephen Pope
Kevin Pope
John Pope
Audrey V. Pope
Henry Power

Paul Pope
Denis Pope
Martin Pope
John Anthony Pope
Stephen Pope
Robert Thomas Pope
Therese Potts

Michael Quirk
Julie Quirk
Lawrence Quirk

Patricia Quirk (nee Kehlenbeck)
Joanne Quirk

Elizabeth Reoch
Mary Rimmer
Colin James Ritchie
Margaret Patricia Robinson
Mary Rogers (nee Blundell)
Phillip Rogers

Clare Rimmer
Sarah Ritchie
John Edward Robinson
Stanley Rogers
John Rogers
Margaret Ronson

Elizabeth Small
Ann Smith
Veronica Summers
Sheila Swanson
Caroline Swanson

Mary Small
Henry Smith
John Swanson
John Martin Swanson
Maureen Swanson

Joseph Tapper
Veronica C. Tierney
Patricia Ann Torpey
Anna Tumilty
Jane Tumilty

Margarey Tapper
Arthur Hilary Torpey
Tom Treanor
Andrew Tumilty
Peter Tumilty

Patricia Varney

Austin Varney

Maureen Waddell
Peter White
Hannah White
Brenda White
Hester Mary Whitlock Blundell
Susan Williams (nee Kehlenbeck)
Ruth Williams

Frances White (nee Kehlenbeck)
Lucie White
James White
Brian Mark Whitlock Blundell
Charles Williams
Cheryl Williams

Robert Joseph Williams   Both interred in churchyard.
Ellen Ann Williams (nee Rafferty) (Loving parents of Derek and Daughter in law Pat.)
Vernon Williams   Rita Mary Williams
Anthony Vernon Williams   Kevin Hugh Williams
John Wills   Anne Wills
Mary Wilson   Janet Wilson
Terence Wiseman   Irene Wiseman
Elizabeth Wiseman   James Wright (R.I.P.)
Margaret Wright (R.I.P.)   James Wright
Maureen Wright   John Wright
Michael Wright   Helen Wright
Moira Wright   Thomas Wright
Jane Wright   Andrew Wright
Nicholas Wright   Robert Vincent Wright
John Joseph Wright   Jean Margaret Wright

Lord thou hast been our refuge from generation to generation. Look upon thy servants and upon their works, and direct their children. And let the brightness of the Lord our God be upon us.

Psalm 90.

CHAPTER 5

Wars, Laws and Renewal.

Notes

(1) B. Plumb, *Found Worthy* (Warrington 1986).

(2) Plumb.

(3) Crosby Hall: Archives.

(4) L. Albertini, *The Origins of the War of 1914* (Oxford 1952).

(5) B.M. Whitlock Blundell, *Francis Nicholas Blundell 1884 - 1936* (Ms Crosby Hall).

(6) F.N.B.; *The Tablet*, 31 January, 1920.

(7) F.N.B.

(8) F.N.B.

(9) F.N.B.

(10) Crosby Hall: Archives; Plumb, *Found Worthy.*

(11) F. Tyrer, *The History of the R.C. Church, Little Crosby.* (pp174, Ms Crosby Library, 1956).

(12) F. Tyrer, *St. Mary's Church, Little Crosby* (Farnworth 1983) pp15 - 25.

(13) F.N.B.

(14) W.S. Churchill, *The Second World War* (London 1948) Vol 1, p44; Personal interview with Miss Teresa Jones, 18 March, 1997.

(15) Personal recollections.

(16) *Cathedral Record*, September 1947.

(17) Crosby Hall: Archives.

(18) *Cathedral Record,* February 1951. November 1952 to February 1953; Personal interview with Mrs. Christine Watson, 14 March, 1997, with Mrs. Mollie Gilligan, 18 March, 1997 and with Mr. Bob Wright, 24 April, 1997.

(19) P. Hebblethwaite, *John XXIII Pope of the Council,* (London 1984); J.C. Heenan, *A Crown of Thorns An Autobiography 1951 - 1963.* (London 1974).

(20) A.C.F. Beales 'The Struggle for the Schools' in *The English Catholics* (London 1950); Universe, 5 June, 1959 p4.

(21) B. Plumb, *The Catholic Historians Handbook 1829 - 1965.* (Wigan 1995) p3; Personal Interview with Mrs. M.C. Barnes, 24 April, 1997 and with Mr. Bob Wright on the same day.

(22) Information from the Benedictine Year Book.

(23) Crosby Hall Centre publicity brochure.

(24) Information supplied by Mgr. Sidney Breen, 14 March, 1997; *Liverpool Archdiocesan Directory 1994.*

(25) Personal Interviews 14 March, 18 April, 24 April, 1 May 1997.

APPENDIX 1

Harkirk Burial Register

1. 7 April 1611 ffirst of all Wm. Mathewson, an ould man of ye Morehowses within little crosbie, a Catholicke - denyed buriall at Sephton Churche by the parson thereof.
2. 10 April 1611 Ellen Blundell, the wyffe of Thomas Blundell of ye Carrhowses in Ince blundell, denyed buriall at Sephton as aforesaid.
3. 9 May, 1611 Margerie Rigat of muche Crosbie, denyed etc.
4. 6 ffebr. 1612 Edward Tyrer of muche Crosbie, denyed etc.
5. 6 Sept. 1612 Ric. Holland - of ye Halle of Sutton in ye pishe Prescot.
6. 2 Oct. 1612 Grace Marrowe, wyffe of John Cadicke, of muche Crosbie - denyed etc.
7. 28 Nov. 1612 Richarde Ryding of ye Morehowses within litle Crosbie - denyed etc.
8. 30 Nov. 1612 Margerie, widowe of Richard Ryding being likewise denyed burial etc.
9. Dec. 1612 Richarde Tarleton of ffazakerley, gent. buried uppo Saturday night.
10. 16 May, 1613 Wm. Tarleton of litle Crosbie, husbandman, a Catholicke.
11. 23 April, 1613 Jane Barone, ye widowe of Wm. Thomason of Carrhowses in Ince Blundell, the Parson refusing etc.
12. 31 August, 1613 John Synett an Irishman borne in Wexforde, master of a barke, was excommunicated by the B. of Chester for being a Catholicke recusant - -
13. 3 October, 1613 Raphe Croft of litle Crosbie, a Catholicke Recusant, denyed etc.
14. 11 Nov. 1613 Anne Lawrence, daughter of ye wyffe of Humphrey Lunt of Ince Blundell - denyed etc.
15. 24 Dec. 1613 John Saterthwait P.(riest) buried in ye Harkirche on Christenmas eve at or about 8 o'clocke in the evening.
16. 28 Feb. 1614 Elizabeth ye widowe of Rich. Smith of Ince Blundell dyed a Catholicke therefore denyed etc.
17. 10 March 1614m Charite Melling, an ould woman and daughter of Richard Melling - of Ayntree, dyed there a Catholicke, denyed buriall bothe at Melling Chappell and at Sephton Churche.
18. 1 July, 1614 Jane Snopson, widow and syster of Margaret Barker of Darbie, widowe dying a Catholicke.
19. 25 July, 1614 Margerie Davison, a servant maide at ye Grange, dyed there a Catholicke, denyed etc.
20. 2 Dec. 1614 Margarette, ye wyffe of Henrie Blundell of Ince Blundell (who dwelt at ye Grange) dyed a Catholicke - denyed etc.
21. 3 Jan. 1615 Catherine ye widowe of Tho. Patrike als Gorton, litle Crosbie - a Catholicke, denyed etc.
22. 20 May, 1615 Anne ye wyffe of George Webster of Liverpoole (tenant to Mr. Crosse) denyed buriall at ye Chappell of Liverpoole by ye Curate and by ye Maior and by Mr. Moore.
23. 27 October 1615 Margaret ye wyffe of Thomas Newhouse of Thornton - denyed etc.
24. 27 Apr. 1616 Ellen Melling, daughter of John Melling of Incebl. a Catholicke.

25. 17 Sept. 1616 Thomas Blundell of the Carresyde in Ince Blundell, a Catholicke.
26. 13 Oct. 1616 Anne Blundell, sister to Thomas Blundell of the Morehowses and wyffe to Thomas Holme of Dounholland, a Catholicke, with her litle infant by her.
27. 13 Oct. 1616 Margaret, ye widowe of Raphe Crosse, a Catholicke denyed etc.
28. 11 Dec. 1616 Emline, wyffe of John Glover, denyed etc.
29. 16 Dec. 1616 Wm. Moneley of Holmore greene, Smith, denyed etc.
30. 4 Febr. 1617 John Cadicke of muche Crosbie denyed etc.
31. 9 Oct. 1617 Ellen ye wyffe of Richarde Johnson denyed etc.
32. 10 Oct. 1617 John Marrow of litle Crosbie, denyed etc.
33. 23 Jan. 1618 Wm. Nicholasson als Davit of litle Crosbie, denyed etc.
34. 28 Jan. 1618 Ellen, ye wyffe of Richard Johnson of ye Morehowses, denyed etc.
35. 3 Mar. 1618 Henrie Blundell of late dwelling in ye Morehowses and about ye age of 100 yeares, a Catholicke denyed etc.
36. 27 Aug. 1618 Ellen ye wyffe of John Longroe, denyed etc.
37. 29 Jan.1619 Catherine ye widowe of John Rigate, neare ye Chappell of much Crosbie, denyed etc.
38. 18 Sept. 1619 Humphrey Wetherbie of the Lunt, denyed etc.
39. 11 Feb. 1619 (sic) Elizabeth, late widowe of Robte. Blundell, Saler, denyed etc.
40. 27 Feb. 1620 John Birtwisell P.(riest) buried in the night about 2 of the clocke.
41. 6 May, 1620 Edwarde Suthworth of ye more lain, denyed etc.
42. 28 Sep. 1620 Ales Rigate, ye wyffe of John Rothwell, denyed etc.
43. 1 Nov. 1620 Anne, widowe of Richard Worrall, denyed etc.
44. 4 Sep. 1620 (sic) Margaret Sumner, denyed etc.
45. 9 Jan. 1621 Robert Rothwell, denyed etc.
46. 8 Mar. 1621 John Davie an infant of James Davie.
47. 21 Apr. 1621 Another young infant, daughter of Mr. Wake.
48. 22 May, 1621 Ann, widowe of Bryan Ley, refused by ye Parson etc. In this space was buried 2 infants of Thomas Blundell of ye Morehowses, 1 of Thomas Holmes of Dounholland, 2 of Richard Bryanson of ye Morehowses, 1 of Richard Marrowe's of litle Crosbie, viz. 6.
55. 28 Mar. 1622 Ellen, ye widowe of Richarde Blundell of ye Morehowses, denyed etc.
56. Sinch wch tyme hath been buried an Infant of James Davies.
57. 31 July, 1622 John Worthington P.(riest).
58. 15 Nov. 1622 James Ryse of ye Morehowses, denyed etc.
59. 16 Febr. 1623 James Whitmore (younger Sonne of John Whitmore of Thursington in Worrall, Esq., a great and zealous Catholicke and Confessor etc.) dyed at ye Edge, denyed buriall etc.
60. 16 Mar. 1623 Elizabeth, ye wyffe of Oswald Hill of Ince Blundell, denyed etc.
61. 2 June, 1623 Agnes, the widow of Richard Ryse of litle Crosbie, denyed etc.
62. 12 June, 1623 Alice Harrison, als Johns daughter, ye widowe of Hughe Johnson, buried 12 of June being the feast of Corpus Christi 1623, denyed etc.
63. 14 June, 1623 Elizabeth, wyffe of Raphe Starkey, denyed etc.
64. 22 Oct. 1623 Ales, ye widowe of Wm. Nicholasson als Davie, denyed etc.
65. 1 Jan. 1624 Jane Lunt, widowe of Edward Lunt of muche Crosbie, denyed etc.
66. 28 Jan. 1624 Anne Worrall, wyffe of John Thompson of ye Morehowses, denyed etc.

67. 4 Febr. 1624 Ales Bootle, wyffe of Wm. Cooke of Orrell, denyed etc.
68. 5 Febr. 1624 Anne Atherton, wyffe of James Dawbie, not buried at ye Churche because shee dyed a Catholicke.
69. 19 Febr. 1624 John Laiton P.(riest) buried about 9 of the Clocke at night.
70. 19 Mar. 1624 Robte. Blundell, borne at ye Carre-syde, and a long time blind, dyed in Liverpoole, denyed etc.
71. 1 July, 1624 Margaret Valentyne, daughter of Richard Valentyne als Phillipot of Bickerstaffe, was according to her desyre buried here.
72. 15 Oct. 1624 Thomas Arnolde, borne in litle Crosbie, denyed etc.
73. 2 Febr. 1625 Ales Newhouse late wyffe of James Tarleton of Holmore greene, denyed etc.
74. 10 May, 1625 Elizabeth, widowe of James Ryse of the Morehowses, refused etc.
75. 22 May, 1625 Elizabeth, widow of John Lurting of muche Crosbie, denyed etc.
76. 26 Nov. 1625 James Arnold, an Innocent sonne of Wm. Arnold of litle Crosbie, denyed etc.
77. 14 Mar. 1624 (sic) Anne, wyffe of John Nicholassone of muche Crosbie, refused etc.
78. 9 Apr. 1626 Ellen, daughter of John Rise of litle Crosbie and wyffe of Richarde Shepparde of muche Crosbie, refused etc.
79. 17 May, 1626 Elizabeth, widowe of Edward Suthworth, denyed buriall by Parson as all others were.
80. 27 May, 1626 William Raban P.(riest), buried at night.
81. 19 Oct. 1626 Marie Newhouse ye widowe of William Rogerson, denyed etc.
82. In this space was buried twoe children of Richard Blundell of the Carrsyde.
84. 6 May, 1627 Elizabeth, wydowe of Richard Ballarde of Ince, dying a Catholicke Recusant denyed etc.
85. 29 June, 1627 Bridget wyffe of Thomas Griffith of muche Crosbie, Catholic Recusant, denyed etc.
86. 29 Dec. 1627 John Nicholasson of muche Crosbie, being overseene with drinke (as it was thought) was drowned in a pitte. Parson of Sefton would not etc.
87. 8 Jan. 1628 Oswalde Hogg, Catholicke Recusant, stilo novo Romano.
88. 9 Jan. 1628 John Burghe a Catholicke, denyed etc.
90. 3 Mar. 1628 James Dawbie of ye Morehowses, denyed etc. Stilo Romano.
91. 28 Maii, 1628 John Reignolde of the Northend, a Catholicke Recusant, denyed etc.
92. 7 July, 1628 Peter Stocke of litle Crosbie, yeoman, Catholique Recusant.
93. 18 August, 1628 Margarett the widowe of Oswalde Hogge, a Catholicke, therefore etc.
94. 4 Octo. 1628 Jane Mellinge, widowe, buried at 9 of ye Clocke at night.
95. 17 Octo. 1628 Ann, the wyffe of Wm. Worrall of Litherland, denyed etc.
96. 3 Dec. Cecilie, the wyffe of Peter Rydinge of the Morehowses.
97. 23 Jan. 1629 Agnes, wyffe of Robert Rydinge of Sephton towne, denyed etc., buried after the Romane Accompt.
98. 2 Feb. 1629 Catherine Rydinge, daughter of Peter Rydinge of the Morehowses, denyed etc.
99. 8 Feb. 1629 Jane Cropp, servant to Wm. Abram of Thornton, dying a Catholique etc.

100. 17 Feb. 1629 Elizabeth, daughter to Master Richard Holland of Sutton, the wyffe of Robte. Bootle of Hoolmore in Thornton, denyed etc., buried three of the clocke in the morning after the Roman Accompt.

101. 7 March, 1629 Wm. Tarleton of Orrell, husbandman, a Catholique recusant, buried at night, stilo romano.

102. 9 March, 1629 George Rydinge, sonne of Peter Rydinge of the Morehowses. Stylo Romano.

103. 16 March, 1629 Margerie, widowe of John Marrowe of litle Crosbie. Stylo Romano.

104. 5 Maie, 1629 Ellen, widow of Raphe Willmson of Ince Blundell. Stylo Romano. She was the last person to be denied burial at Sefton Church.

105. 26 April, 1633 John Mellings P.(riest) buried in the evening. (He was commonly called Maxfield).

106. 19 Sept. 1634 Richard Home P.(riest) buried at ten of the Clocke at night. (He was called Smith).

107. 29 October, 1634 Richard Robteson P.(riest) buried about 2 of the Clocke after midnight.

108. Ralph Melling, Priest. 2 May 1660.

109. Thomas Fazakerley, Priest, son of Mr. Rob. Fazakerley of Spellow House, dyed at Croxteth, March 22 1664 - 5.

110. Alexander Barker, Priest, dyed 11 October, 1665 in Little Crosby. He went by the name of Parre.

111. John Beesley, Priest, dyed March 30, 1674. He was commonly called Mollins.

112. John Birtwistle, Priest, dyed January ye 26, 1680 at Croxteth, buried early in ye morning.

113. Mr. Thomas Martin, born at Goran near Kilkenny, died at Croxteth having been chaplain to ye Lord Molyneux, buried 11 June, 1691.

114. Mr. Tho. Eccleston, borne in Great Singleton in ye Fylde in Lancashire, was a Clergie Priest, spent more yn. 40 years in assisting poore Christias in ye parishes of Halsall and Aughton, buried in ye Harkirk, Ano. 1700.

115. Mr. Richard Barton.

116. Tho. Blundell, y 3rd son of William Blundell, Esq. deceased, dyed at Litham, Mr. Clifton's house on Wednesday ye 27 May, 1702. His body was carried to Crosby and buried in ye Harkirk on ye 29. He was a learned man, aged 55. Religious and of good life. He entered ye Society of Jesus anno 1666. This is written by ye hand of W.B. his Broth'r.

117. Mr. Edward Molyneux, bourn at Alt Grange, killed by a faule off his horse.....Buried ye 29 April A.D. 1704 about tenn of ye Clocke at night.

118. Mr. Rich. Foster was born in Sutton; came from Prage to be a Missioner in these parts, chiefly at Formby; he lived at ye Newhouse in ye Car houses in Ince and dyed ye 9 May, An. 1707. Buried next to Mr. Ed. M.

119. Mrs. Frances Blundell, doughter to Nicholas Blundell and Great Aunt to me Nicho. Blundell, dyed in ye 81 year of her age, Dec. ye 2nd, 1711. Buried ye day following in ye Harkirk; she never married; she dyed at Ormskirk; she had lived at Crosby ye Greatest part of her life.

120. Mr. Henry Tasburgh a Priest of ye Society of Jesus, dyed at ye New House, January 27, 1718. Buried next to Mr. Foster in ye Harkirk.

121. Mr. George Lovell a Priest of ye Society of Jesus, a virtuous and good Man and a very great Mathematission, was a Missior in Lancashire, most of his Time with Bartholemew Walmesley of Dungen Hall, Esq, but becoming a perfect Child and having lost his memory he was kept for some time at ye New House in Ince, where he dyed December ye 12, 1720.

122. Mr. Robert Aldred was born in London, he was a Priest of the Society of Jesus; he came to live with me, August ye 6th. A.D. 1707, and continued with me for som years, then lived as my Priest at Edward Howerds in Little Crosby till the West lain Hous was built for him where he dyed Febr. ye 23, A.D. 1727 - 8 and was buried in the Harkirk on ye 25; he was a Laborious good Missioner, a Fastious plesant man, and very well beloved by Protestants as well as Catholicks; he lyes next to Mr. Lovell on this nearer side of him.

123. Mr. William Pinnington, Priest of the Society of Jesus, born at Salford by Manchester, a zealous Missioner, seven years with Marchall Tallard when Prisoner at Nottingham (he being French General); he Laboured under Great Distempers with exemplary Patience after a long illness, a sort of coadjutor to Mr. Carpenter of Liverpool; he dyed there the 8th of June, 1736.

124. Mary Harrison dyed Octo. 24, 1736. She was born in Cleton near Preston; was never married, housekeeper to Mr. Clifton at Westlane house in Little Crosby (where she dyed). Her death much lamented by all the neighbours and the whole Congregation.

125. Grace Tootell, wife to Hugh Tootell of Brindle, came to the Hall of Crosby to see her son Hugh who was Butler there, and sick. She fell ill and Dyed. Buried in the Harkirk next to Miss Frances Blundell, April 6th, 1737.

125.(sic) Mr. Francis Williams, priest of the Society of Jesus, died at Ince Blundell.

126. Servant to Mr. Molinx who is priest at Moor Hall, dyed at Great Crosby.

127. Jane Rostron, servant to Mr. Clifton at the Westlane house; she dyed at sd. house the 21 of Aug. 1740.

128. Jane Formby, servant to Mr. Clifton of New ho. dyed - 1745, buryd in the Harkk.

129. Mr. William Clifton, Priest, S.J. dyed the 18 of August, 1749 abt. 5 in ye morning at New House in Ince Blundell.

130. Mr. James Clifton, Priest, S.J. who lived about 20 years at Westlane ho. in Little Crosby, and nephew of the forgoing dyed at sd. house abt. 3 o'clock on Thursday morn. 27 Septr, 1750. He was a very laborious good Missioner, and much regretted by the neighbrs to whom he was very usefull in regard to their Souls and bodily infirmities.

131. Mr. Peter Williams, S.J. dyed 26 November, 1753 at Ince Blundell.

APPENDIX 2

Episcopal Certificate of Consecration of St. Mary's Church, with translation.
(The original is kept in the parish archives).

MDCCCXLVII die septima mensis Septembris
Ego Georgius Episcopus Floensis Vicarius Apostolicus Districtus
Lancastriensis in Anglia consecravi Ecclesiam e altare
hoc in honore Beatae Mariae semper Virginis et Reliquas
sanctorum Martyrum Thomae Cantuariensis Episcopi Sanctae Philomenae
Virginis et Martyris et Sanctae Teresiae Virginis in eo inclusi,
et singulis Christi fidelibus hodie unum annum et in die anniversario
consecrationis huius- modi ipsum visitantibus quadraginta dies vera
indulgentia in forma Ecclesiae consueta concesse.
GEORGIUS EPISCOPUS FLOENSIS
VICAR APOSTOLICUS

On the 7 September 1847, I, George, Bishop of Floensis,
Vicar Apostolic of the Lancashire District in England
consecrated the church and this altar in honour of the
Blessed Mary ever Virgin and placed in it the relics of the
holy Martyrs Thomas of Canterbury, Bishop, St Philomena,
Virgin and Martyr and St Teresa, Virgin, and grant to each
individual faithful who visits the church this day one year
true indulgence and to those who visit the church on the
anniversary of its consecration forty days true indulgence in
accordance with the custom of the Church.

The Friends of St Mary's, Little Crosby, wish to acknowledge the support given by Barry Coyne of Coyne Brothers, Funeral Directors, in the publication of this history of St Mary's Church and the village of Little Crosby.